I, Tituba, Black Witch of Salem

CARAF Books
Caribbean and African Literature
Translated from French

Carrol F. Coates, Editor

Clarisse Zimra, J. Michael Dash, John Conteh-Morgan,
and Elisabeth Mudimbe-Boyi, Advisory Editors

I, Tituba,
Black Witch of Salem

Maryse Condé

Translated by Richard Philcox
Foreword by Angela Y. Davis
Afterword by Ann Armstrong Scarboro

University of Virginia Press
CHARLOTTESVILLE

University of Virginia Press
Originally published as *Moi, Tituba, sorcière* . . . *Noire de Salem*
by Maryse Condé, © Editions Mercure de France, 1986
This translation and edition © 1992 by the Rector and
Visitors of the University of Virginia

First published 1992
First paperback edition published 2009
ISBN 978-0-8139-2767-1 (paper)

3 5 7 9 8 6 4

The Library of Congress has cataloged the hardcover
edition as follows:

Library of Congress Cataloging-in-Publication Data

Condé, Maryse.
[Moi, Tituba, sorcière. English]
I, Tituba, Black witch of Salem / Maryse Condé ; translated by
Richard Philcox ; foreword by Angela Y. Davis ; afterword by Ann
Armstrong Scarboro.
p. cm. —(CARAF Books)
Translation of: Moi, Tituba, sorcière.
Includes bibliographical references (p.).
ISBN 0-8139-1398-5
1. Tituba—Fiction. 2. Witchcraft—Massachusetts—Salem—
History—Fiction. 3. Salem (Mass.)—History—Colonial period,
ca. 1600–1775—Fiction. I. Title. II. Series.
PQ3949.2.C65M5613   1992
843—dc20   92-8134
CIP

Tituba and I lived for a year on the closest of terms. During our endless conversations she told me things she had confided to nobody else.

MARYSE CONDÉ

———————

Death is a porte whereby we pass to joye;
Lyfe is a lake that drowneth all in payne.

JOHN HARRINGTON

Contents

Foreword

I can look for my story among
the witches of Salem, but it isn't there.

Tituba's impassioned efforts to revoke her own disappearance from history—Maryse Condé's fictional re-vision of her story—is Tituba's revenge. Throughout her life, she recoils before the prospect of exacting revenge, for fear of becoming like those who are responsible for her misery. This transcendant revenge—the retelling of a history that is as much mine as it is hers—allows her to save herself without taking on the historical characteristics of the colonizers and the slaveholders she detested.

Tituba looked for her story in the history of the Salem witch trials and could not find it. I have looked for my history in the story of the colonization of this continent and I have found silences, omissions, distortions, and fleeting, enigmatic insinuations. Tituba's quest for recorded evidence of her existence as a living, feeling, loving, active individual, who was as much a part of the Salem witch trials as her codefendants of European descent, leads her to a belittling, cursory allusion: "Tituba, a slave originating from the West Indies and probably practicing 'hoodoo.'" She counters this footnote that condemns her to insignificance with a strong, self-affirming "I, Tituba . . . Witch." Maryse Condé lends her the words that assist her to tell you and me her story, speaking her life in her own voice—from the womb to the realm of the dead.

Maryse Condé's historical novel about the black witch of Salem furnishes Tituba with a social consciousness as contemporary as the motivating impulse behind the novel, which drives Condé to retrieve fragments of an intentionally ignored history and to reshape them into a coherent, meaningful story. It is the same consciousness that has motivated contemporary women of African descent—both scholars and artists—to explore the infinite possibilities of our lost history.

As Condé offers to Tituba the possibility of filling the silence and voids with voice and presence, we who are Tituba's cultural kin experience the possibilities of our own history. Via an active, constitutive voice, Tituba leaps into history, shattering all the racist and misogynist misconceptions that have defined the place of black women. Tituba's revenge consists in having persuaded one of her descendants to rewrite her moment in history in her own African oral tradition. And when Tituba takes her place in the history of the Salem witch trials, the recorded history of that era—and indeed the entire history of the colonization process—is revealed to be seriously flawed.

Tituba's voice is her own. Maryse Condé even tells us in a prefatory remark that "Tituba and I lived for a year on the closest of terms. During our endless conversations she told me things she had confided to nobody else." But, of course, Condé meticulously researched this historical person, and Tituba's voice is infused with the historically complex and imaginative voice of her creator. It is therefore not rigidly anchored to the social issues of Tituba's times. This historical novel refuses to be confined within the ideological limits of the era during which it unfolds. Tituba engages in recurring meditations on her relationship—as a black woman—to feminism. In this sense, her voice can be viewed as the voice of a suppressed black feminist tradition, one that women of African descent are presently reconstituting—in fiction, criticism, history, and popular culture.

Tituba is a powerfully sexual being. She accepts and embraces her sexuality and does not allow the strong sexual attraction she feels for men to dilute her active solidarity with women, black as well as white. Yet, because of her defense of her sexuality, she is reluctant to call herself a feminist. From our contemporary vantage point, feminists of all cultures may find enlightenment in her ambivalence.

Tituba is conceived during a violent rape on a slave ship heading toward Barbados. She spends her formative years on the margins of slave society in Barbados, learning the African art of healing and ancestor reverence and, what is certainly not a contradiction, the spiritual wonderment of sexual love. It is because of her dedication to the ways of her ancestors—and the use of her healing powers to help the women of the family that owns her—that she becomes a target of the Salem witch hunt. Having survived that terrifying ordeal, she returns to Barbados, where she dies as a revolutionary.

This is one possible version of Tituba, the black witch of Salem. There are those who dispute her African descent, countering that she was Indian, perhaps hoping to stir up enmity between black and Native American women as we seek to re-create our respective histories. As an African-American feminist, I offer my profound gratitude to Maryse Condé for having pursued and developed her vision of Tituba, Caribbean woman of African descent. Should a Native American Tituba be re-created, in scholarly or fictional terms, this would be true to the spirit of Condé's Tituba and her revenge. For, in the final analysis, Tituba's revenge consists in reminding us all that the doors to our suppressed cultural histories are still ajar. If we are courageous enough to peer through the narrow openings, we will discover our fears, our rage, our hopes, and our roots. And sometimes there is magic behind those doors, sparkling clues about the possibilities ahead.

ANGELA Y. DAVIS

Acknowledgments

I could not have written this essay without the extensive coopera-
tion of Maryse Condé herself. I am also grateful to Richard Philcox,
Maryse's husband and my friend, for his aid in recording the May
1991 interview. Finally, I am deeply indebted to Jim Arnold for
sharing his expertise in both editing and literary criticism.

AAS

The translator wishes to acknowledge the assistance of Ann Armstrong Scarboro and Viviane Johnson.

RP

Preparation of this volume was made possible by a translation grant
from the National Endowment for the Humanities.

AJA

I

I

Abena, my mother, was raped by an English sailor on the deck of *Christ the King* one day in the year 16** while the ship was sailing for Barbados. I was born from this act of aggression. From this act of hatred and contempt.

When we arrived many weeks later at the port of Bridgetown, nobody noticed my mother's condition. As she could not have been more than sixteen years old at the time and was beautiful to behold with her jet black skin and high cheekbones subtly marked with tribal scars, a rich planter by the name of Darnell Davis bought her for a good deal of money. He also bought two male slaves, Ashantis as well, victims of the tribal wars between their people and the Fantis. He put my mother in the service of his wife, who never ceased to pine for England and whose mental and physical condition required constant attention. He believed that my mother would know how to entertain her with songs, possibly dances, and those devices he thought the slaves to be particularly fond of. He set the two men to work on his flourishing sugarcane plantation and in his tobacco fields.

Jennifer, Darnell Davis's wife, was not much older than my mother. She hated this brute she had been forced to marry and who had already fathered a horde of illegitimate children. He would leave her alone in the evenings while he went drinking. Jennifer and my mother became friends. After all, they were little more than two children frightened by the roar of animals in the night and the shadow play of the flamboyant, calabash, and silk-cotton trees on the plantation. They slept together, and while she played with the long plaits of her mistress's hair, my mother would tell her the stories that her mother had told her in the village of Akwapim, where she was born. She would conjure up all the forces of nature at their bedside in order to appease the darkness and to prevent the vampires from draining them white before dawn.

When Darnell Davis saw that my mother was with child, he went into a rage at the thought of all those pounds sterling he had spent to buy her. Now he was going to be burdened with a woman in ill health and of no use whatsoever! He refused to give in to Jennifer's entreaties, and to punish my mother he gave her to Yao, one of the Ashantis he had bought in the same batch, while forbidding her to set foot in the Great House. Yao was a young warrior who could not resign himself to planting, cutting, and grinding sugarcane. Twice he had tried to kill himself by swallowing poisonous roots. Twice he had been saved at the last minute and brought back to the life he hated. By offering him a concubine, Darnell hoped he would be giving him a taste for life and thereby get a return for his money. What a bad idea it had been to go to the slave market in Bridgetown that morning of June 16**! One of the two men had died. The other was suicidal. And Abena was pregnant!

My mother stepped into Yao's cabin shortly before the evening meal. He was lying on his bedding, too depressed to think of food, and he hardly glanced at the woman who had been announced.

When Abena appeared, he sat up and murmured: "*Akwaba!*" Then he recognized her. "It's you!" he exclaimed.

Abena burst into tears. Too many storm clouds had gathered over her short life: her village had been burned to the ground, her parents had been stabbed to death trying to defend themselves, she had been raped, and now she had to endure this brutal separation from Jennifer, a creature as gentle and desperate as herself.

Yao stood up, his head touching the ceiling, for he was as tall as a silk-cotton tree. "Don't cry. I won't touch you. I won't harm you. We speak the same language don't we? We worship the same gods." Then he lowered his eyes. "It's the master's child, isn't it?"

Abena shed still hotter tears of shame and grief. "No, no, it isn't! But it's a white man's child even so."

While Abena stood there in front of him with her head hung low, Yao's heart filled with immense compassion. It seemed to him that this child's humiliation symbolized the condition of his entire people: defeated, dispersed, and auctioned off. He wiped away the tears that were running down her face. "Don't cry. From now on your child is mine. Do you understand? And just let someone try and say it isn't!"

She kept on crying, so he lifted her head up and asked: "Do you know the story of the bird who laughed at the leaves of the palm tree?"

My mother gave a faint smile. "Who doesn't? When I was small it was my favorite story. My grandmother used to tell it to me every evening."

"Mine too . . . And the one about the monkey who wanted to be the king of animals? And he climbed up to the top of the silk-cotton tree so that they would all bow down in front of him. But one of the branches broke and he found himself on the ground with his ass in the dust."

My mother laughed. She hadn't laughed for months. Yao took the bundle she was holding and put it in a corner of the cabin.

"The place is filthy," he apologized, "because I'd lost all interest in living. For me it was like a puddle of dirty water you try to avoid. Now that you are here, everything's going to be different."

They spent the night in each other's arms, like brother and sister, or rather like father and daughter, chaste and affectionate. A week went by before they made love.

When I was born four months later, Yao and my mother were in a state of happiness. That sad, uncertain happiness of being a slave, constantly under threat, and making do with intangible scraps! At six o'clock every morning, with his cutlass slung over his shoulder, Yao set off for the fields and took his place in the long line of men in rags trudging along the footpaths. In the meantime my mother grew tomatoes, okra, and other vegetables in her plot of ground, cooked, and kept some skinny chickens. At six o'clock in the evening the men would return home and the women would fuss over them.

My mother sorely regretted that I was not a boy. It seemed to her that a woman's fate was even more painful than a man's. In order to free themselves from their condition, didn't they have to submit to the will of those very men who kept them in bondage and to sleep with them? Yao, on the other hand, was delighted. He took me in his big bony hands and anointed my forehead with the blood of a chicken, after having buried my mother's placenta under a silk-cotton tree. Then, holding me up by the feet, he presented me to the four corners of the horizon. It was he who gave me my name: Tituba. TI-TU-BA. It's not an Ashanti name. Yao probably invented it to prove that I was the daughter of his will and imagination. Daughter of his love.

The first years of my life were spent peacefully. I was a beautiful, chubby baby, and my mother's milk did wonders for me. Then I learned to talk and walk. I discovered the sad, yet wonderful universe around me. The slave cabins made of dried mud, silhouetted against the huge sky, the haphazard arrangement of plants and trees, the sea and its bitter song of freedom. Yao turned my face toward the open sea and whispered in my ear: "One day we shall be free and we shall fly back to the country we came from." Then he rubbed my body with a knot of dried seaweed to stop me from getting yaws.

In actual fact Yao had two children, my mother and me. For my mother, he was much more than a lover: he was a father, a savior, and a refuge.

When did I discover that my mother did not love me? Perhaps when I was five or six years old. Although the color of my skin was far from being light and my hair was crinkly all over, I never stopped reminding my mother of the white sailor who had raped her on the deck of *Christ the King*, while surrounded by a circle of obscene voyeurs. I constantly reminded her of the pain and humiliation. So whenever I used to cuddle up to her, as children are wont to do, she would inevitably push me away. Whenever I would throw my arms around her neck, she would quickly duck her head. She listened only to what Yao told her to do. "Sit her on your lap. Kiss her! Fondle her!"

Yet I did not suffer from this lack of affection, because Yao's love was worth the love of two. My tiny fingers nestled in his hard, rough hand. My tiny foot in his enormous footprint and my forehead in the hollow of his neck. Life had a kind of sweetness about it. Although it was forbidden by Darnell, in the evenings the men would mount their tall drums and the women would lift their rags up on their glistening legs and dance!

Several times, however, I witnessed scenes of brutality and torture. I saw men go home covered in blood, their chests and backs striped in scarlet. I even saw one of them die under my very eyes, vomiting a violet froth of blood. They buried him at the foot of a majagua tree. Then everyone rejoiced because at least one of us had been delivered and was on his way home.

Motherhood, and especially Yao's love, had transformed my mother. She was now a young woman, as lithe and purple as the sugarcane flower. Her eyes shone from under the white kerchief she tied about her forehead. One day she took me by the hand to go and dig up the yam patch in a plot of ground the master had given to the slaves. A breeze was blowing the clouds out to sea and the sky had been washed a soft blue. My Barbados is a flat island with a few hills dotted here and there.

We had started off along a footpath that wound through the Guinea grass when suddenly we heard the sound of angry voices. It was Darnell reprimanding an overseer. At the sight of my mother, his expression changed radically and flickered between surprise and delight. "Is that you, Abena?" he exclaimed. "Well, the husband I gave you is doing wonders for you. Come over here."

My mother stepped back so sharply that the basket on her head holding a cutlass and a calabash of water fell to the ground. The calabash broke into three pieces, spilling its contents over the grass. The cutlass stuck upright in the ground, icy and murderous, while the basket started to roll down the path as if it were fleeing the drama that was about to unfold. Terrified, I ran after the basket and managed to catch it.

When I turned back toward my mother, she was standing up

against a calabash tree, breathing hard. Darnell stood less than three feet away. He had taken off his shirt, undone his trousers, and I could see his very white underclothes. His left hand was groping for his penis. Turning her head in my direction, my mother screamed: "The cutlass! Give me the cutlass!"

I obeyed as quickly as I could, holding the enormous blade in my tiny hands. My mother struck two blows. The white linen shirt slowly turned scarlet.

*   *   *

They hanged my mother.

I watched her body swing from the lower branches of a silk-cotton tree. She had committed a crime for which there is no pardon. She had struck a white man. She had not killed him, however. In her clumsy rage she had only managed to gash his shoulder.

They hanged my mother.

All the slaves had been summoned to her execution. Once her neck had been broken and her soul had departed, there rose up a clamor of anger and revolt that the overseers silenced with great lashes of their whips. Taking refuge in one of the women's skirts, I felt something harden inside me like lava; a feeling that was never to leave me, a mixture of terror and mourning.

They hanged my mother.

When her body swung round and round in the air, I gathered up enough strength to tiptoe away and vomit my heart out in the grass.

In order to punish Yao for his concubine's crime, Darnell sold him to a planter by the name of John Inglewood, who lived on the other side of Mount Hillaby. Yao never arrived at his destination. On the way there he committed suicide by swallowing his tongue.

As for me, I was driven off the plantation by Darnell at the tender age of seven. I would probably have died if it hadn't been for that almost sacred tradition of solidarity among slaves.

An old woman took me in. As she had seen her man and two sons tortured to death for instigating a slave revolt, she seemed to act deranged. In fact, she was hardly of this world and lived constantly in their company. She had cultivated to a fine art the ability to communicate with the invisible. She was not an Ashanti like my mother and Yao, but a Nago from the coast, whose name, Yetunde, had been creolized into Mama Yaya. People were afraid of her, but they came from far and wide because of her powers.

She started off by giving me a bath of foul-smelling roots, letting the water run over my arms and legs. Then she had me drink a potion of her own concoction and tied a string of little red stones around my neck. "You will suffer during your life. A lot. A lot." She uttered these terrifying words perfectly calmly, almost with a smile. "But you'll survive." That was not very reassuring! But the hunched and wrinkled figure of Mama Yaya gave off such an air of authority that I did not dare protest.

Mama Yaya taught me about herbs. Those for inducing sleep. Those for healing wounds and ulcers. Those for loosening the tongues of thieves. Those that calm epileptics and plunge them into blissful rest. Those that put words of hope on the lips of the angry, the desperate, and the suicidal.

Mama Yaya taught me to listen to the wind rising and to measure its force as it swirled above the cabins it had the power to crush.

Mama Yaya taught me the sea, the mountains, and the hills. She taught me that everything lives, has a soul, and breathes. That everything must be respected. That man is not the master riding through his kingdom on horseback.

One day I fell asleep in the middle of the afternoon. It was the dry season. The slaves were chanting plaintively as they hoed and cut in the stifling heat. Then I saw my mother. Not the disjointed, tormented puppet swinging round and round among the leaves, but decked out in the colors of Yao's love.

"Mother!" I cried.

She came and took me in her arms. God! How sweet her lips were! "Forgive me for thinking I didn't love you. Now I know I'll never leave you," she said.

"And Yao? Where is Yao?" I cried out in happiness.

She turned around. "He's here too." And Yao appeared.

I ran to tell my dream to Mama Yaya, who was peeling the

tubers for the evening meal. She smiled knowingly. "Do you really think it was a dream?" I remained dumbfounded.

From that moment on Mama Yaya initiated me into the upper spheres of knowledge. The dead only die if they die in our hearts. They live on if we cherish them and honor their memory, if we place their favorite delicacies in life on their graves, and if we kneel down regularly to commune with them. They are all around us, eager for attention, eager for affection. A few words are enough to conjure them back and to have their invisible bodies pressed against ours in their eagerness to make themselves useful. But beware of irritating them, for they never forgive and they pursue with implacable hatred those who have offended them, even in error. Mama Yaya taught me the prayers, the rites, and the propitiatory gestures. She taught me how to change myself into a bird on a branch, into an insect in the dry grass or a frog croaking in the mud of the River Ormond whenever I was tired of the shape I had been given at birth. And then she taught me the sacrifices. Blood and milk, the essential liquids. Alas! shortly after my fourteenth birthday her body followed the law of nature. I did not cry when I buried her. I knew I was not alone and that three spirits were now watching over me.

It was at this juncture that Darnell sold the plantation. A few years earlier his wife, Jennifer, had died leaving him a frail, pale baby son, who was periodically shaken with fever. Despite the copious milk he received from a slave, who had been forced to give up nursing her own son, he seemed destined for the grave. Darnell's paternal instinct was aroused for his only white offspring and he decided to return to England to try and cure him.

The new master bought the land without the slaves, which was not at all the custom. With their feet in chains and a rope around their necks, they were taken to Bridgetown to find a buyer. Then they were scattered to the four corners of the island, father separated from son and mother from daughter. Since I no longer belonged to Darnell and was a squatter on the plantation, I was not part of the sad procession that set off for the slave market. I knew a spot on the edge of the River

Ormond where nobody ever went because the soil was marshy and not suitable for growing sugarcane. With the strength of my own hands I managed to build a cabin on stilts. I patiently grafted strips of earth and laid out a garden where soon all sorts of plants were growing, placed in the ground with ritual respect for the sun and air.

Today I realize that these were the happiest moments of my life. I was never alone, because my invisible spirits were all around me, yet they never oppressed me with their presence.

Mama Yaya put the finishing touches to her lessons about herbs. Under her guidance I attempted bold hybrids, cross-breeding the *passiflorinde* with the *prune taureau*, the poisonous *pomme cythère* with the surette, and the *azalée-des-azalées* with the *persulfureuse*. I devised drugs and potions whose powers I strengthened with incantations.

In the evening the violet sky of the island stretched above my head like a huge handkerchief against which the stars sparkled one by one. In the morning the sun cupped its hand in front of its mouth and called for me to roam in its company. I was far from men, and especially white men. I was happy. Alas! all that was to change.

One day a great gust of wind blew down the chicken house and I had to set off in search of my hens and handsome scarlet-necked rooster, straying far from the boundaries I had set for myself.

At a crossroads I met some slaves taking a cart of sugarcane to the mill. What a sorry sight! Haggard faces, mud-colored rags, arms and legs worn to the bone, and hair reddened from malnutrition. Helping his father drive the oxen was a boy of ten, as somber and taciturn as an adult who has lost faith in everything.

The minute they saw me, everybody jumped into the grass and knelt down, while half a dozen pairs of respectful, yet terrified eyes looked up at me. I was taken aback. What stories had they woven about me? Why did they seem to be afraid of me? I should have thought they would have felt sorry for me instead, me the daughter of a hanged woman and a recluse who lived alone on the edge of a pond. I realized that they were mainly thinking about my connection with Mama Yaya, whom they had feared. But hadn't Mama Yaya used her powers to do good? Again and again? The terror of these people seemed like an injustice to me. They should have greeted me with shouts of joy and welcome and presented me with a list of illnesses that I would have tried my utmost to cure. I was born to heal, not to frighten.

I went home sadly, with no further thought for my hens and my rooster, who by now must have been crowing in the grass along the highway. This meeting was to have lasting consequences. From that day on I drew closer to the plantations so that my true self could be known. Tituba must be loved! To think that I scared people; I who felt inside me nothing but tenderness and compassion. Oh yes, I should have liked to unleash the wind like a dog from his kennel so that the white Great Houses of the masters would be blown away over the horizon, to order a fire to kindle and fan its flames so that the whole island would be purified and devastated. But I didn't have such powers. I only knew how to offer consolation.

Gradually the slaves got used to seeing me and came up to me, at first shyly, then with more confidence. I visited the cabins and comforted the sick and dying.

2

"Hey! Are you Tituba? It's not surprising people are afraid of you. Have you looked at yourself recently?"

The speaker was a young man much older than I was, since he could not have been less than twenty, tall, skinny, light-skinned, and with curiously smooth hair. When I tried to reply, the words flew away as if they were unwilling to talk and I couldn't put two of them together to make a sentence. In my great confusion I let out a groan that sent the young man into fits of laughter.

"No, it's not surprising people are afraid of you," he repeated. "You don't know how to talk and your hair is a tangle. You could be lovely if you wanted to."

He came up boldly. If I had been more used to contact with men, I would have seen the fear in his eyes that constantly moved like a rabbit's and were just as bronze. But I didn't and I was simply fascinated by the bravado of his voice and his smile.

"Yes, I am Tituba. And you, who are you?" I finally managed to answer.

"They call me John Indian."

It was an unusual name and I frowned. "Indian?"

He puffed himself up. "My father was, they say, one of the last remaining Arawak Indians that the English couldn't budge. He was an eight-foot giant. He had me with a Nago woman he used to visit in the evenings and here I am, another little bastard on his long list."

He spun round again in a burst of laughter. His gaiety struck me. So there were people who were happy on this wretched earth!

"Are you a slave?" I stammered.

"Yes," he nodded. "I belong to Goodwife Susanna Endicott who lives over there in Carlisle Bay." He pointed to the sea glistening in the distance. "She sent me to buy some Leghorn eggs from Samuel Waterman."

"Who is Samuel Waterman?" I asked.

He laughed. Once again the laughter of someone with no inhibitions. "Don't you know he's the one who bought the plantation from Darnell Davis?" And thereupon he bent down and picked up a round basket he had placed at his feet. "Well, I must be off now. Otherwise I'll be late and Goodwife Endicott will start prattling again. You know how women like to prattle. Especially when they start getting old and haven't got a husband."

All this talk made my head spin. As he moved off with a wave of his hand, I don't know what came over me, but I said in a tone of voice I had never heard myself use before: "Will I see you again?"

He stared at me. I wonder what he saw in my face. "Sunday afternoon there's a dance at Carlisle Bay," he swaggered. "Do you want to come? I'll be there."

I jerked my head up and down.

I slowly went back to my cabin. I saw the place I called home with new eyes and it looked sinister. The planks, roughly squared off with an axe, were blackened by wind and rain. The purple flowers of a giant bougainvillea growing against the left side of the cabin did little to brighten it up. I looked around me: a gnarled calabash tree and some reeds. I shuddered. I went over to what remained of the chicken house and grabbed one of the few chickens that had remained faithful to me. With an expert hand I slit open its belly, letting the blood moisten the earth. Then I softly called: "Mama Yaya. Mama Yaya."

She appeared quickly. Not in her mortal shape of a woman of many years, but in the one she had donned for eternity: perfumed and crowned with orange blossom.

"Mama Yaya," I said, panting. "I want this man to love me."

She shook her head. "Men do not love. They possess. They subjugate."

"Yao loved Abena," I protested.

"He was one of the rare exceptions."

"Perhaps John'll be one, too."

She threw back her head so as to let out a snort of incredulity. "They say that this cock has coupled with half the hens in Carlisle Bay."

"I want it to stop!"

"I only have to take one look at him to see he's a shallow nigger, full of hot air and bravado." Then after observing the urgency in my eyes, she said quietly: "All right, go to this dance in Carlisle Bay he's invited you to and carefully get a little of his blood on a piece of cloth. Bring it to me together with something that has been in contact with his skin." And she moved away, but not before I noticed an expression of sadness on her face. She had probably seen the pattern of my life start to unfold. Like a river that can never be fully diverted from its course.

Up until now I had never thought about my body. Was I beautiful? Was I ugly? I had no idea. What had he said? "You know, you could be lovely." But he had been such a joker. Perhaps he was laughing at me. I took off my clothes, lay down, and let my hand stray over my body. It seemed to me that these curves and protuberances were harmonious. As I neared my pudenda, it seemed that it was no longer me but John Indian who was caressing me. Out of the depths of my body gushed a pungent tidal wave that flooded my thighs.

I could hear myself moan in the night.

Was that how my mother had moaned in spite of herself when the sailor had raped her? I understood then why she had wanted to spare her body the second humiliation of a loveless possession and had tried to kill Darnell. What else had he said? "Your hair is in a tangle." The next morning when I awoke I went down to the River Ormond and cut my mop of hair as best I could. As the last woolly locks fell into the water I heard a sigh. It was my mother. I hadn't called her, but I understood that an imminent danger had brought her out of the invisible world.

"Why can't women do without men?" she groaned. "Now you're going to be dragged off to the other side of the water."

Surprised, I interrupted her. "To the other side of the water?"

But she said no more, merely repeating in a distressed voice: "Why can't women do without men?"

Mama Yaya's reluctance, and my mother's lamentations, might have warned me to take care. But this was not the case. On Sunday I set off for Carlisle Bay.

In a chest I had discovered a mauve calico dress and a percale skirt that must have belonged to my mother. As I slipped the clothes on, two creole-style earrings rolled to the ground. I winked at the invisible spirit.

The last time I had been to Bridgetown was when my mother was alive. Almost ten years had gone by, and the town had grown tremendously. It had become an important seaport. A forest of masts hid the bay and I could see flags of all nationalities flying. The wooden houses looked elegant to me with their verandas and enormous roofs, their windows open wide like the eyes of a child.

I had no trouble finding the dance, as the music could be heard a long way off. If I had had some notion of time I would have known it was carnival, the only season of the year when the slaves were free to enjoy themselves. So they came in from all corners of the island to try and forget they were no longer human beings. People were looking at me and I heard them whisper: "Where does she come from?"

Obviously nobody thought there was any connection between this elegant young person and the half-legendary Tituba whose deeds were related from plantation to plantation.

John Indian was dancing with a tall yellow girl with a pleated madras head tie. He left her high and dry in the middle of the dance floor and came over to me, his eyes sparkling like those of his Arawak ancestor.

"You came," he laughed. "You actually came." Then he took me by the arm. "Come on, come on."

"I can't dance," I protested.

He burst out laughing again. My God how this man could laugh! And as each note rang out, a locked compartment burst open in my heart.

"A Negress who can't dance? Have you ever heard of such a thing!"

Black Witch of Salem

Soon there was a circle around us. Wings grew on my ankles and heels. My hips and waist became supple. A mysterious serpent had entered me. Was it the primordial snake that Mama Yaya talked about so much, in the form of god the creator of all things on the surface of the earth? Or was it he who was making me sway? Sometimes the tall yellow girl with the pleated madras head tie attempted to come between John Indian and me. We ignored her. At one point John Indian wiped his forehead with a large seersucker handkerchief, and I remembered Mama Yaya's words: "A drop of his blood. Something that has come into contact with his skin."

For a moment my head started to spin. Was it really necessary to go through with this since he seemed "naturally" attracted to me? Then I had the intuition that the main thing was not so much to attract a man as to keep him, and that John Indian must belong to the species that is easily attracted but has no intention of making any lasting commitment. I therefore obeyed Mama Yaya.

I scratched his little finger while I carefully stole his handkerchief.

"Ow! What are you doing, little witch?"

He was joking, but it made me think. What is a witch? I noticed that when he said the word, it was marked with disapproval. Why should that be? Why? Isn't the ability to communicate with the invisible world, to keep constant links with the dead, to care for others and heal, a superior gift of nature that inspires respect, admiration, and gratitude? Consequently, shouldn't the witch (if that's what the person who has this gift is to be called) be cherished and revered rather than feared? All these thoughts made me morose and I left the room after one more polka. John Indian was too busy to notice I had left. Outside, the black cord of night was strangling the island. Not a breath of air. The trees were motionless, like stakes. I recalled my mother's lament: "Why can't women do without men?" Yes why?

※　※　※

"I'm not a bush nigger, a maroon! I'll never come and live in that rabbit hutch of yours up in the woods. If you want to live with me you'll have to come to my home in Bridgetown."

"Your home?" I laughed disparagingly and added: "Since when does a slave have a 'home'? Don't you belong to Susanna Endicott?"

He seemed annoyed. "Yes, I belong to Susanna Endicott, but she's a good mistress. . . ."

I interrupted him. "How can a mistress be 'good'? Can a slave cherish his master?"

He pretended not to have heard and went on: "My house is behind hers and I do what I like there." He took me by the hand. "Tituba, you know what they say about you, they say you're a witch!" That word again! "I want to prove to everyone that it's not true and take you openly as my woman. We'll go to church together, I'll teach you the prayers."

I knew I should have fled. Instead, I stayed rooted to the spot, passive and adoring.

"Do you know the prayers?" I shook my head. "How the world was created on the seventh day? How our father Adam was turned out of the earthly paradise through the fault of our mother, Eve?"

What strange story was this he was telling? But I didn't have the strength to protest. I withdrew my hand and turned my back.

"Tituba, don't you want me?" he whispered against my neck.

And therein lay my misfortune. I wanted that man as I had never wanted anyone else. I desired his love as I had never desired any other. Not even my mother's. I wanted him to touch me. I wanted him to caress me. I was merely waiting for the moment when he would take me and the valves of my body would open wide, flooding me with pleasure.

He went on whispering against my skin: "Don't you want to live with me from the time the silly roosters puff themselves up in the farmyard until the sun sinks into the sea and the ardent hours begin?"

I had the strength to get up. "It's a serious matter. Let me think about it for a week and I'll bring you my answer on this very same spot."

In a rage he picked up his straw hat. What was there about John Indian to make me sick with love for him? Not very tall, average height, five feet seven, not very big, not ugly, not hand-some either! A fine set of teeth, burning eyes. I must confess it was downright hypocritical of me to ask myself such a question, since I knew all too well where his main asset lay and I dared not look below the jute cord that held up his short, tight-fitting *konoko* trousers to the huge bump of his penis.

"Until Sunday then," I said.

I had barely arrived home when I called Mama Yaya, who was in no hurry to listen to me and appeared with a frown on her face.

"What do you want now? Haven't you got all you wanted? He's asking you to live with him."

"You know very well that I don't want to return to the white man's world," I said very quietly.

"There's no way of escaping it."

"Why? Why?" I almost shouted. "Can't you bring him here? Do you mean to say there's a limit to your powers?"

Instead of getting angry, she looked at me with tender compassion. "I have always told you. The universe has its rules that I cannot entirely change. Otherwise I would destroy this world and build another where our people would be free. Free to enslave the white men in their turn. Alas! I cannot."

I could think of nothing in reply and Mama Yaya disappeared as she had come, leaving behind her that perfume of eucalyptus peculiar to the invisible world. Left alone, I lit the fire between four stones, wedged in my earthenware pot, and threw a hot pepper and a piece of salt pork into the water to make a stew. And yet I didn't feel like eating.

My mother had been raped by a white man. She had been hanged because of a white man. I had seen his tongue quiver out of his mouth, his penis turgid and violet. My adoptive father had committed suicide because of a white man. Despite all that, I was considering living among white men again, in their midst, under their domination. And all because of an uncontrollable desire for a mortal man. Wasn't it madness? Madness and betrayal?

That night, and for seven more nights and days, I struggled with myself. In the end, I confessed I was beaten. I wouldn't want anyone to go through the agony I went through. Remorse. Shame. Panic. Fear.

On the following Sunday I packed a few of my mother's dresses and three petticoats into a wicker basket. I wedged a pole against the door of my house. I set my animals free. The hens and the guinea fowl that had given me their eggs. The cow that had given me her milk. The pig that I had been fattening for a year without ever having the heart to kill it.

I murmured a long prayer for the dwellers of this place I was abandoning. Then I set off for Carlisle Bay.

Susanna Endicott was a small woman of about fifty, with graying hair that was parted in the middle and brushed up into such a tight chignon that it pulled back the skin on her forehead and temples. I could read all the aversion she had for me in her eyes, which were the color of sea water. She stared at me as if I were an object of disgust.

"Tituba? Where did that name come from?"

"My father gave it to me," I replied coldly.

She turned purple. "Lower your eyes when you speak to me."

I obeyed for the love of John Indian.

"Are you a Christian?" she went on.

John Indian hastily intervened. "I'm going to teach her the prayers, Mistress! And I'm going to see the vicar of Bridgetown so that she can be baptized as soon as possible."

Susanna Endicott stared at me again. "You will clean the house. Once a week you will scrub the floor. You will do the washing and ironing. But you will leave the cooking to me. I cannot bear to have you niggers touching my food with the discolored, waxy palms of your hands."

I looked at my palms. Gray and pink like a seashell. Whereas John Indian greeted this outburst with a roar of laughter, I remained dumbfounded. Nobody had ever spoken to me, humiliated me, in such a manner!

"You can go now!"

John started to hop from one foot to another and in a whining, humble voice, like a child asking for a favor, he pleaded: "Mistress, when a nigger takes a wife doesn't he deserve two days rest? Doesn't he, Mistress?"

Susanna Endicott spat and her eyes were now the color of

stormy seas. "A nice woman you've got yourself there and pray God you don't repent it!"

John Indian burst out laughing again and between two peals of laughter, cried: "Pray God! Pray God!"

Susanna Endicott suddenly softened her tone. "Be off with you and report back to me on Tuesday."

In the same comical and exaggerated way, John insisted: "Two days, Mistress! Two days!"

"All right, you've won," she burst out. "As always! Report back Wednesday. But don't forget it's the day the post comes."

"Have I ever forgotten?" he said proudly. Then he threw himself on the ground to seize her hand and kiss it.

Instead of letting him have his way she struck him across the face. "Get out of here, nigger!"

My blood was boiling inside me.

John Indian, who knew what I was thinking, started to hurry me away when Susanna's voice nailed us to the spot. "Well, Tituba, aren't you going to thank me?"

John squeezed my fingers as if to crush them.

I managed to murmur a weak: "Thank you, Mistress."

Susanna Endicott was the widow of a rich planter, one of the first to have learned the Dutch art of extracting sugar from cane. On the death of her husband she had sold the plantation and freed all the slaves, since, because of a paradox I couldn't understand, although she hated Negroes, she was strongly opposed to slavery. Only John Indian remained in her household where he had been brought up ever since he was a baby. Susanna Endicott's beautiful and spacious home in Carlisle Bay stretched out amidst a wooded park; at the bottom stood John Indian's little house, which, I must confess, I found quite attractive with its lime-plastered wattling and a small-columned veranda hung with a hammock.

John Indian closed the door with a wooden latch and took me in his arms, whispering: "The duty of a slave is to survive! Do you understand? To survive!"

His words reminded me of Mama Yaya and tears started to run down my cheeks. John Indian drank them one by one, trailing their salty trickle to the inside of my mouth. I choked. I could not forget the pain and shame I felt at his behavior in front of Susanna Endicott, but my rage sharpened my desire for him. I bit him savagely at the base of his neck. He gave one of his magnificent laughs and shouted: "Come, my little wild mare, let me tame you."

He picked me up and took me into the bedroom, which had a four-poster bed—an unexpected baroque fortress—right in the middle. Finding myself on this bed, which Susanna Endicott had probably given him, unleashed my fury and our first moments of love-making resembled a battle.

I expected a lot from these moments and I was not disappointed. When I turned on my side, exhausted and in search of sleep, I heard a bitter sigh. It was probably my mother, but I refused to communicate with her.

Those two days were an enchantment. Neither rigid nor complaining, John Indian was used to doing everything for himself and he treated me like a goddess. It was he who kneaded the corn bread, prepared the stew, and sliced the avocados, the pink-fleshed guavas, and the slightly overripe-smelling pawpaws. He brought me food in bed in a calabash with a spoon he had carved himself and had decorated with triangular motifs. He told me stories, parading around in the midst of an imaginary circle of listeners.

"*Crick, crack.* Is the court awake?"

He untied my hair and did it up his own way. He rubbed my body with coconut oil perfumed with ylang-ylang.

But those two days only lasted two days. Not one hour longer. On Wednesday morning Susanna Endicott hammered on the door and we heard her shrewish voice cry out: "John Indian, do you remember it's post day? And there you are lying in bed with your wife!"

John sprang out of bed. I dressed more slowly. When I arrived at the house Susanna Endicott was having her breakfast in the kitchen. A bowl of gruel and a slice of black bread. She pointed to a circular object on the wall and asked: "Can you read the time?"

"Time?"

"Yes, wretch, that is a clock. And you start work at six o'clock every morning."

Then she showed me a bucket, a broom, and a scrubbing brush. "To work!"

The house had twelve rooms, plus an attic piled high with leather trunks containing the clothes of the late Joseph Endicott. Apparently he had liked fine linen.

When I went back downstairs, tottering from exhaustion with my dress soiled and wet through, Susanna Endicott was having tea with her friends, half a dozen women like herself, their skin the color of curdled milk, their hair drawn back, and the ends of their shawls knotted around their waists. Their multicolored eyes stared at me in fright.

"Where did she come from?"

"She's John Indian's woman," said Susanna Endicott in a tone of mock solemnity.

The ladies all exclaimed at once and one of them protested: "Under your roof! In my opinion, Susanna Endicott, you give that boy too much liberty. You forget he's a nigger."

Susanna Endicott shrugged her shoulders indulgently. "Well, it's better that he has all he needs at home rather than running all over the island wearing himself out sowing his wild oats."

"I hope she's a Christian at least."

"John Indian is going to teach her her prayers."

"And are you going to let them marry?"

It was not so much the conversation that amazed and revolted me as their way of going about it. You would think I wasn't standing there at the threshold of the room. They were talking about me and yet ignoring me. They were striking me off the map of human beings. I was a nonbeing. Invisible. More invisible than the unseen, who at least have powers that everyone fears. Tituba only existed insofar as these women let her exist. It was atrocious. Tituba became ugly, coarse, and inferior because they willed her so. I went out into the garden and heard their comments, which proved they had inspected me from head to foot while pretending to ignore me.

"She has eyes that turn your blood cold."

"The eyes of a witch. Susanna Endicott, do be careful."

I went back to the cabin and sat down on the veranda, over-whelmed. After a while I heard a sigh. It was my mother again. This time I turned to her and said savagely: "Weren't you ever in love when you were on this earth?"

She nodded. "But he didn't degrade me. On the contrary. Yao's love gave me respect and faith in myself."

Thereupon she curled up at the foot of a bush of wild roses. I didn't move. All I needed to do was get up, take my small bundle of clothes, close the door behind me, and set off back toward the River Ormond. Alas! It was impossible.

The slaves who flocked off the ships in droves and whose gait, features, and carriage the good people of Bridgetown mocked were far freer than I was. For the slaves had not chosen their chains. They had not walked of their own accord toward a raging, awe-inspiring sea to give themselves up to the slave dealers and bend their backs to the branding iron.

That is exactly what I had done.

*   *   *

"I believe in God, the Father Almighty, Maker of Heaven and Earth, and in Jesus Christ, his only son, Our Lord . . ."

I shook my head frantically. "John Indian, I can't repeat this."

"Repeat, my love. What matters for the slave is to survive. Repeat, my angel. You don't think that I believe in their story of the Holy Trinity? One God in three distinct persons? But it doesn't matter. You just need to pretend. Repeat!"

"I can't!"

"Repeat, my love, my little mare with a tousled mane. What matters most is that we are together in this big bed like a raft on the rapids."

"I can't. I've forgotten."

"I promise you, my love, my angel, this is all that counts. So repeat after me."

John Indian joined my hands forcibly together and I repeated after him: "I believe in God, the Father Almighty, Maker of Heaven and Earth . . ."

But these words meant nothing to me. They had nothing in

common with what Mama Yaya had taught me.

As she did not trust John Indian, Susanna Endicott herself undertook to have me recite my catechism lessons and to explain the words of her Holy Bible. Every afternoon at four, there she was with her hands folded on a thick leather-bound volume that she would not open before crossing herself and murmuring a short prayer. I remained standing in front of her and tried to find the correct words.

For it is difficult to explain the effect that woman had on me. She paralyzed me. She terrified me.

Her eyes, the color of sea water, made me lose my bearings. I was reduced to what she wanted me to be: a gawk of a girl with skin of a repulsive color. In vain I called those who loved me to the rescue, but they were of no help. When I was far from Susanna Endicott I reprimanded myself, I reproached myself and swore to stand up to her at our next tête-à-tête. I even devised impertinent and insolent answers to defeat her questions. Alas! Once I was back in front of her, my confidence always failed me.

One day I pushed open the door of the kitchen where she sat waiting for our lessons and immediately her look told me quietly that she had a lethal weapon she was about to use on me. The lesson, however, started as usual. I courageously launched into: "I believe in God, the Father Almighty, Maker . . ."

She did not interrupt me. She let me stammer and stutter and trip up over the slippery English syllables. When I had finished my recitation, as breathless as if I had run up a hill, she said: "Aren't you the daughter of that Abena who killed a planter?"

"She didn't kill him, Mistress," I protested. "Just wounded him."

Susanna Endicott smiled as if all these niceties bore little weight and went on. "Weren't you brought up by a certain Nago witch called Mama Yaya?"

"Witch," I stammered. "Witch? She took care of people and cured them."

She smiled knowingly and her thin, colorless lips fluttered. "Does John Indian know about all this?"

"What is there to hide?" I managed to retort.

Her eyes dropped back to her book. At that moment John Indian came in carrying the wood for the kitchen and saw me so distressed that he realized something terrible was brewing. Alas! It wasn't until long afterward that I was able to tell him. "She knows! She knows who I am!"

His body became stiff and cold like a day-old corpse. "What did she say?" he murmured.

I told him everything and he murmured frantically: "Not a year ago Governor Dutton had two slaves who had been accused of dealing with Satan burned in the square at Bridgetown. For the whites that's what being a witch means. . . !"

"Dealing with Satan!" I objected. "Before setting foot inside this house I didn't know who Satan was!"

"Go and tell that to the court!" he sneered.

"The court?"

John Indian was so terrified that I could hear his heart beat in the room.

"Tell me!" I ordered him.

"You don't know the whites. If she manages to get them to believe that you're a witch, they'll build a stake and put you on it!"

That night, for the first time since we had lived together, John Indian did not make love to me. I tossed and turned by his side, groping for the object that had given me so much pleasure. But he pushed me away.

The night wore on. I heard the wind howl through the palm trees. I heard the swell of the sea. I heard the bark of the dogs, trained to smell out slave prowlers. I heard the din of the cocks announcing the daylight. Then John Indian got up and without a word locked up in his clothes the body he had refused me. I burst into tears.

When I entered the kitchen to start my daily chores, Susanna Endicott was deep in conversation with Betsey Ingersoll, the minister's wife. I knew they were talking about me, for their heads almost touched above the steam rising from their bowls of gruel. John Indian was right. A plot was being woven.

In court the word of a slave, even a freed slave, did not count. I could bawl and shout as much as I liked that I didn't know

I, Tituba

who Satan was, nobody would listen to me. So I made up my mind to protect myself. Without further ado.

I stepped out into the afternoon heat at three o'clock, oblivious of the sun. I went down to the plot of ground behind John Indian's house and sank into prayer. There was not room enough in this world for Susanna Endicott and me. One of us had to go and it wasn't going to be me.

4

"I've spent the whole night calling you! Why are you only getting here now?"

"I was at the other end of the island, comforting a slave whose man died under torture. They whipped him. They rubbed hot pepper on his wounds and then they tore off his penis."

This story, which at another time would have revolted me, left me indifferent. I went on passionately: "I want her to die slowly, suffering horribly, knowing it's because of me."

Mama Yaya shook her head. "Don't let yourself be eaten up by revenge. Use your powers to serve your own people and heal them."

"But she has declared war on me," I protested. "She wants to take John Indian away from me."

Mama Yaya laughed sadly. "You'll lose him anyway."

"What do you mean?" I stammered.

As if she had nothing to add to what she had just let slip, Mama Yaya did not answer. Seeing me distraught, my mother, who had heard the conversation, said softly: "A fine loss that would be! That nigger will get you into no end of trouble!" Mama Yaya looked at her disapprovingly and she said no more.

I chose to ignore her words and turned to Mama Yaya. "Will you help me?"

My mother spoke again. "Hot air and bravado! That nigger is nothing but hot air and bravado!"

Finally, Mama Yaya shrugged her shoulders. "And what do you want me to do? Haven't I taught you everything I possibly could? Besides, soon I won't be able to be of any help."

I resigned myself to looking squarely at the truth and asked: "What do you mean?"

"I'll be so far away. It'll take so long to cross the water. And it'll be so difficult . . ."

"Why will you have to cross the water?"

My mother burst into tears. Amazing! This woman, who when she was alive treated me with so little affection, was now becoming almost overprotective in the other world! A little exasperated, I purposefully turned my back on her and repeated: "Mama Yaya, why will you have to cross the water to see me?"

Mama Yaya did not answer and I understood that, whatever her affection for me, my mortal condition obliged her to keep a certain reserve.

I accepted this silence and returned to my previous preoccupations. "I want Susanna Endicott to die!"

My mother and Mama Yaya both got up together. Mama Yaya said wearily: "Even if she does die you cannot change your fate. And you will have perverted your heart into the bargain. You will have become like them, knowing only how to kill and destroy. Strike her instead with an inconvenient and humiliating sickness."

The two shapes disappeared and I remained alone to meditate on my next move. An inconvenient and humiliating sickness? Which one would I choose? When dusk brought John Indian home, I had not reached a decision. He seemed cured of his fright and he even brought me a surprise: a mauve velvet ribbon, bought from an English trader, which he fixed in my hair himself. I recalled the pessimistic words of Mama Yaya and Abena, my mother, concerning him and I wanted to reassure myself.

"John Indian, do you love me?"

"More than my own life," he cooed. "More than that God Susanna Endicott keeps going on about. But I also fear you."

"Why do you fear me?"

"Because I know you are violent. I often see you as a hurricane ravaging the island, laying flat the coconut palms and raising the lead-gray waves up to the sky."

"Be quiet! Make love to me!"

Two days later Susanna Endicott was taken with a violent cramp while she was serving tea to the minister's wife. The latter scarcely had time to step outside and call John Indian, who was chopping wood, before a malodorous liquid streamed down the mistress's legs and formed a frothy puddle on the floor. They called for Dr. Fox, a man of science who had studied at Oxford and published a book entitled *Wonders of the Invisible World*. The choice of such a doctor was by no means unintentional. Susanna Endicott's sickness was too sudden not to arouse suspicion. Only the day before she had been teaching the children their catechism with her shawl tied tightly around her firm waist and her hair covered with a hood. Only the day before she had marked with a blue cross the eggs that John Indian had been sent to sell at the market. Perhaps she had already made known her suspicions about me. Whatever the case, Fox came and examined her from head to foot. If he was repelled by the terrible stench that rose from her bed, he did not show it. He stayed closeted with her for almost three hours. When he came down, I heard him jabbering with the minister and some of his followers.

"I have found in no secret part of her body either large or small growths where the devil could have suckled her. Likewise, I have found neither red nor blue spots similar to a flea bite. And still less painless marks that when stuck with a pin do not bleed. I can therefore make no positive conclusion."

How I would have liked to witness the decomposition of my enemy, now a soiled baby wrapped in dirty linen. But nothing could be glimpsed through her door that was opened just wide enough to let one of her loyal friends scamper up and down with trays and chamber pots.

As the saying goes: "When the cat's away, the mice they will play."

The Saturday after Susanna Endicott took to her bed, John Indian began to play. I knew he wasn't like me, a morose creature, brought up all alone by an old woman, but I had no idea he had so many friends. They came from everywhere, even from the faraway parishes of St. Lucy and St. Philip. One slave had taken two days to walk from Cobblers Rock. The tall yellow girl in the pleated madras head tie was also one of the guests. She merely threw me an angry look without coming near, as if she understood who was the stronger. One of the men had carried off from his master's shop a barrel of rum, which they opened with a mallet. After two or three goblets had been passed from hand to hand, things started to liven up. A black Congo slave, who resembled a gnarled wooden pole, jumped up onto the table and began to shout riddles.

"Listen to me, men. Listen closely. I am neither king nor queen. And yet I make the world shake."

"Rum, rum!" the audience roared.

"Although I'm tiny, I can light up a cabin."

"A candle, a candle!"

"I sent Mathilda for the bread. The bread arrived before Mathilda did."

"Coconut, coconut!"

I was terrified, unused to such noisy outbursts, and a little disgusted by the promiscuity. John Indian took me by the arm. "Don't put on such a face, or my friends will think you're condescending. They'll say your skin is black, but you're wearing a white mask over it."

"It's not that," I whispered. "But what if someone hears all your noise and comes to see what's going on?"

"And so what?" he laughed. "They expect niggers to get drunk and dance and make merry once their masters have turned their backs. Let's play at being perfect niggers."

I did not find that amusing, but without more ado he spun around and launched into a boisterous mazurka.

The highlight of the party occurred when some of the slaves slipped inside the house where Susanna Endicott was stewing in her urine and came back with an armful of clothes that had belonged to her late husband. They put the clothes on and imitated the solemn and pompous manners of men of his rank. One of the slaves tied a handkerchief around his neck and pretended to be a minister. He pretended to open a book, to leaf through it, and started to chant a litany of obscenities. Everyone split their sides laughing and John Indian most of all. Then the "minister" jumped up on a barrel and thundered: "I am going to marry you, Tituba and John Indian. If anyone knows of any reason why these two should not be brought together, let him come forward and speak."

The tall yellow girl in the pleated madras head tie walked up and raised her hand. "I do! John Indian had two illegitimate children with me as like him as two halfpennies. He promised to marry me!" The comedy could no doubt have turned sour. But nothing of the sort happened. Amidst another burst of laughter the makeshift minister looked inspired and declared: "In Africa where we come from everyone is entitled to his share of women, to as many as his arms can hold. Go in peace, John Indian, and live with your two Negresses."

Everybody clapped hands and someone threw the yellow girl and me up against John Indian, who started to shower both of us with kisses. I pretended to laugh, but I must say that my blood was boiling inside me. Flying off into the arms of another dancer, the yellow girl shouted back: "Men, my dear, are made to be shared!"

I refused to answer and went out onto the veranda.

The revelry lasted until the small hours of the morning. And strangely enough, nobody came and ordered us to be quiet.

* * *

Two days later, Susanna Endicott called John Indian and me to her. She was sitting up in bed with her back against her pillows, her skin already as yellow as her urine, her face haggard but peaceful. The window was open out of respect for visitors and the purifying smell of the sea drowned any fetid vapors. She looked me straight in the eye and once again I could not bear her gaze.

"Tituba," she said, hammering out every syllable, "I know it's one of your spells that has put me in this condition. You are clever enough to outwit Fox and all those who learn their science from books. But you can't deceive me. I want you to know that you may triumph today, but my turn will come tomorrow and I shall get my revenge. I shall get my revenge!"

John Indian started to groan, but she paid no attention to him. Turning to the wall, she let it be known that the conversation was over.

I, Tituba

In the early afternoon a man came to see her, a man such as I had never seen in the streets of Bridgetown, nor for that matter anywhere else. Tall, very tall, dressed in black from head to foot, with a chalky white skin. As he was about to go up the stairs, his eyes fell on me, standing in the half-light with my bucket and broom, and I almost fell over. I have already said much about the eyes of Susanna Endicott, but these! Imagine greenish, cold eyes, scheming and wily, creating evil because they saw it everywhere. It was as if I had come face-to-face with a snake or some other evil, wicked reptile. I was immediately convinced that this Satan we heard so much about must stare in the same way at people he wishes to lead astray.

He spoke and his voice was the same as his look, cold and penetrating: "Negress, why are you looking at me in such a way?"

I scampered off. Then as soon as I had recovered the strength to move, I ran to John Indian, who was sharpening knives on the veranda while humming a beguine. I pressed myself up against him and then finally stammered out: "John Indian, I've just seen Satan!"

He shrugged his shoulders. "Now you're talking like a Christian!" Then, realizing how upset I was, he drew me close and said tenderly: "Satan doesn't like daylight and you won't see him walk in the sun. He's a creature of the night."

The next few hours were torment. For the first time, I cursed my powerlessness, in that my art was lacking much to make it absolutely perfect. Mama Yaya had left this mortal sphere too early to initiate me into the third degree of knowledge, the highest and the most complex. Although I could communicate with the forces of the invisible world and change the present with their help, I was unable to decipher the future. The future remained for me a circular star covered with dense trees whose trunks were so close together they kept out both light and air.

I felt that terrible dangers were threatening me, but I was incapable of naming them and I knew that neither Abena, my mother, nor Mama Yaya could intervene to enlighten me.

That night there was a hurricane. I heard it coming from

a distance, gaining strength and vigor. The silk-cotton tree in the yard tried to resist but gave up around midnight, dropping its topmost branches in a terrible din. As for the banana trees, they lay down meekly and in the morning there was a sight of extraordinary desolation.

This natural chaos made Susanna Endicott's threats even more frightening. Shouldn't I try to undo what I had done, perhaps a little too hastily, and cure a hard-hearted mistress? I was asking myself what to do next when Betsey Ingersoll came to tell us that the mistress was calling for us.

With dread I appeared in front of the shrew. The cunning smile that stretched her colorless lips augured no good. "My death is approaching," she began.

John Indian thought it appropriate to burst into noisy sobs, but she went on without paying him any attention.

"The duty of a master in such cases is to think of the future of those God has put in his charge: his children and his slaves. I have not had the joy of being a mother. But for you, my slaves, I have found a new master."

"A new master, mistress!" John Indian stammered.

"Yes, he's a man of God who will take care of your souls. He's a minister by the name of Samuel Parris. He tried to do business here, but he was unsuccessful. So he is leaving for Boston."

"Boston, mistress?"

"Yes, in the American colonies. Be prepared to follow him."

John Indian was petrified. He had belonged to Susanna Endicott since he was a child. She had taught him to say his prayers and to sign his name. He had been sure that one day or another she would talk of freeing him. But instead of that, here she was telling him that she was going to sell him. And to whom, for God's sake? To an unknown person who was going to cross the sea to seek his fortune in America. In America? Who had ever gone to America?

I myself understood Susanna Endicott's horrible scheme. It was me and me alone she was striking at. It was me she was banishing to America. Me she was separating from my native island, from those who loved me and whose company I needed.

She knew full well what I could retort. She was only too aware of the argument I could use.

"No, Susanna Endicott!" I could retort. "I may be John Indian's woman, but you haven't bought me. You have no deed of ownership listing me with your chairs, your chests of drawers, your bed, and your eiderdowns. So you can't sell me and the gentleman from Boston will not lay hands on my treasures."

Yes, but if I said that, I would be separated from John Indian. Didn't Susanna Endicott excel in cruelty, and of the two of us who was the more formidable? After all, sickness and death are written into our existence and perhaps all I had done was to get them to erupt a little early into Susanna Endicott's life! What was she doing to my life?

John Indian went down on all fours and crawled around the bed. Nothing could be done! Susanna Endicott remained inflexible under her canopy, whose curtains had been drawn open to form a pleated velvet frame.

Mortified and in anguish we went back downstairs.

In the kitchen the minister was talking to a man in front of the fireplace where a vegetable soup was simmering. On hearing our footsteps, the man turned around and in horror I recognized the stranger who had frightened me so much the day before. A horrible foreboding came over me, confirmed by the ruthless violence of his cutting words, spoken in a monotone: "On your knees, dregs of hell! I am your new master! My name is Samuel Parris. Tomorrow, as soon as the sun is up, we shall be leaving aboard the brigantine *Blessing*. My wife, my daughter Betsey, and Abigail, my wife's poor niece, whom we took in upon the death of her parents, are already on board."

5

The new master had me kneel on the deck of the brigantine among the ropes and barrels. The jeering sailors watched as he poured a trickle of icy water on my forehead. Then he ordered me to get up and I followed him to the stern of the vessel where John Indian was standing. He ordered us to kneel beside each other. He came forward and his shadow covered us, blotting out the sun.

"John and Tituba Indian. I hereby declare you man and wife by the holy ties of matrimony to live and remain in peace until death do you part."

"Amen!" stammered John Indian.

I couldn't pronounce a single word. My lips were sealed together. Despite the stifling heat, I was cold. An icy sweat trickled down between my shoulder blades as if I were going to have an attack of malaria, cholera or typhoid. I dared not look in the direction of Samuel Parris, so great was the horror he instilled in me. Around us the sea was a bright blue and the uninterrupted line of the coast, a dark green.

6

I soon realized that someone else shared my fear and aversion for Samuel Parris: Elizabeth, his wife. She was a young woman who was pretty in an odd way. Her lovely blond hair hidden under a somber hood fuzzed up and formed a luminous halo around her head. She was wrapped in shawls and blankets as though she were shivering despite the warm, stuffy air in the cabin. She smiled at me and in a voice as pleasant as the waters of the River Ormond she said: "So you're Tituba? How cruel it must be to be separated from your own family. From your father, your mother, and your people."

Such compassion surprised me. "Fortunately, I have John Indian," I said softly.

Her delicate features expressed revulsion. "You are most fortunate if you believe that a husband can be a pleasing companion and if touching his hand does not send shivers up your spine." There she stopped as if she had said too much.

"Mistress, you don't seem in good health. What are you suffering from?" I asked.

She laughed sadly. "Over twenty physicians have come to my bedside and none has found the cause of my illness. All I know is that my life is a martyrdom. When I stand up, my head spins. I am taken with nausea as if I were pregnant, whereas Heaven has seen fit to grace me with only one child. Sometimes unbearable pains stab my stomach. My menstruation is a torture and my feet are constantly like two blocks of ice."

With a sigh she lay back on the narrow little couch and pulled the coarse woolen blanket up to her neck. I came closer and she motioned to me to sit down next to her.

"How lovely you are, Tituba," she murmured.

"Lovely?" I said it unbelievingly, for the mirror that Susanna Endicott and Samuel Parris had held up for me had convinced me of the opposite. Something gave inside me and impulsively I proposed: "Mistress, let me take care of you!"

She smiled and took my hands. "So many others have tried before you and have failed. But your hands are so soft. As soft as cut flowers."

"Have you ever seen black flowers?" I scoffed.

She thought for a moment and then answered: "No, but if they existed they would be like your hands."

I laid my hand on her forehead, which was curiously cold and damp with sweat. What was she suffering from? I guessed it was the soul that was dragging down the body, as in so many cases of mortal sickness.

At that moment the door was pushed open brutally and Samuel Parris walked in. I couldn't tell who was the more distressed, the more terrified, Mistress Parris or myself.

Samuel Parris did not raise his voice at all. The blood did not flow to his chalky face. He simply said: "Elizabeth, are you mad? Letting this Negress sit next to you. Get out, Tituba, and quick."

I obeyed.

The cold air on deck hit me like a reprimand. How could I let this man treat me like an animal without answering back? I was having second thoughts about it and was on my way back to the cabin when my eyes caught those of two little girls wearing long black gowns that contrasted with their small white aprons. Their brows were capped with hoods, where every wisp of hair had been pushed out of sight. I had never seen children attired in such a fashion. One was the very portrait of the poor recluse I had just left.

"Are you Tituba?" she asked.

I recognized the gracious intonation of her mother.

The other girl, who was two or three years older, stared at me arrogantly.

"Are you the Parris children?" I asked softly.

It was the older of the two who replied. "She's Betsey Parris. I'm Abigail Williams, the minister's niece."

I had not had a childhood. The shadow of my mother's gallows hung over the years that should have been spent in carefree games. For reasons no doubt different from my own, I guessed that Betsey Parris and Abigail Williams had also been robbed of their childhood, dispossessed forever of childhood's natural store of lightheartedness and sweetness. I guessed that nobody had ever sung them lullabies, told them stories, and filled their imagination with wholesome magical adventures. I felt a deep pity for them, especially for little Betsey, who was so charming and vulnerable.

"Come," I said to her. "I'll put you to bed. You look very tired."

The other girl, Abigail, quickly intervened. "What are you talking about? She hasn't said her prayers yet. Do you want my uncle to whip her?"

I shrugged my shoulders and continued on my way.

John Indian was sitting at the stern in the midst of a circle of admiring sailors telling a string of tall tales. Curiously enough, this man who had cried his heart out when our beloved Barbados faded into the mist, was already back to normal. He did a thousand chores for the sailors, earning coins that were used to join in their games and drink their rum. At the moment he was teaching them an old slave song and hollering away with his melodious voice: "*Mougué*, eh, *mougué* eh, cock he sing cock-a-doodle-doo."

Ah, how frivolous was this man my body had chosen! But perhaps I wouldn't have loved him if he too had been cut from a dour cloth of mourning as I had been.

When he saw me he rushed over, abandoning his choir of pupils, who protested noisily. He took me by the arm and whispered: "Our new master is a very strange man. An unsuccessful merchant who decided late to pick up his life where he had left it . . ."

I interrupted him. "I haven't the heart to listen to gossip."

We walked around the deck and took shelter behind a pile of sugar drums bound for the port of Boston. The moon had risen and this timid orb of night gave off as much light as the daystar. I curled up close to John Indian and our hands were searching each other's bodies when a heavy step shook the boards and the drums. It was Samuel Parris. When he observed our position, a little blood filtered into his wan cheeks and he spit out venomously: "I know that the color of your skin is the sign of your damnation, but as long as you are under my roof you will behave as Christians. Come and say your prayers!"

We obeyed. Goodwife Parris and the two girls, Abigail and Betsey, were already on their knees in one of the cabins. The master remained standing, lifted his eyes to the ceiling and started to bray. I couldn't make much out of his speech, except for the oft-heard words sin, evil, Satan, and demon. The most painful moment was the confession. Each of us had to confess out loud his or her sins of the day and I heard the poor children stammer out:

"I watched John Indian dance on the deck."

"I took off my hood and let the sun play with my hair."

In his usual way John Indian confessed to all sorts of tomfoolery and brought it off, since the master merely said to him: "May the Lord forgive you John Indian. Go and sin no more."

When my turn came I was overcome with a kind of rage that was probably nothing else but the other face of the fear Samuel Parris inspired in me, and I said in a firm voice: "Why should I confess? What goes on in my head and my heart is my business."

He struck me. His dry, knifelike hand struck my mouth and made it bleed. At the sight of this red trickle Goodwife Parris regained her strength, sat up, and said in a rage: "Samuel, you have no right . . ."

He struck her in turn. She too bled. This blood sealed our alliance.

Sometimes an arid, desolate soil produces a bloom of sweet colors that perfumes and enhances the surrounding landscape. I can only compare to such a flower the friendship that soon united me with Goodwife Parris and little Betsey. We devised a thousand tricks to be together in the absence of this devil, the Reverend Mr. Parris. I combed their long, blond hair that once freed from the prison of their plaits and buns, fell down to their ankles. I rubbed their pale, unhealthy skins using an oil whose secret Mama Yaya had entrusted to me. Gradually their skin turned golden under my touch.

One day, while I was massaging them, I was bold enough to ask Goodwife Parris: "What does your strict husband think about the change in your body?"

She burst out laughing. "My poor Tituba, how do you expect him to know?"

I raised my eyes upward. "I should have thought nobody was better placed than he is."

She laughed even louder. "If you only knew! He takes me without removing either his clothes or mine, so hurried is he to finish with the hateful act."

"Hateful?" I protested. "For me it's the most beautiful act in the world." She pushed my hand away while I was explaining. "Doesn't it perpetuate life?"

Her eyes filled with horror. "Be quiet! Be quiet! It's Satan's heritage in us." She seemed so upset that I did not take the matter farther.

Usually my conversations with Goodwife Parris did not take this turn. Usually she got enjoyment from the stories that delighted Betsey: those of Anancy the Spider, people who had made a pact with the devil, zombies, *soukougnans,* and the hag who rides along on her three-legged horse. She would listen to me as fervently as her daughter—her beautiful hazel-brown eyes dotted with stars—and ask: "Is that possible Tituba? Can a human being leave his skin and become a spirit miles away?"

I nodded. "Yes, it is possible."

"You must need a broomstick to travel," she argued.

I went into peals of laughter. "What a silly idea! What do you expect to do with a broomstick?"

She remained bewildered. I didn't like it when young Abigail came and disturbed my têtes-à-têtes with Betsey. There was something in that child that made me feel profoundly ill at ease. Her way of looking at me, of listening to me as if I were a frightful and yet bewitching object. She commanded details from me on everything. "What are the words the people in league with the devil have to say before shedding their skin?" "How do the *soukougnans* drink the blood of their victims?"

Black Witch of Salem

My answers were evasive. In truth, I was afraid she would report these conversations to her uncle, Samuel Parris, and that the flicker of pleasure they gave our lives would be snuffed out.

She did nothing of the sort. She possessed an extraordinary faculty for dissimulation. Never at evening prayers did she allude to what in Parris's eyes would have seemed unforgiveable sins. She merely confessed: "I stood on the deck to let the spray fall over me." "I threw half my gruel into the sea."

And Samuel Parris would absolve her: "Go, Abigail Williams, and sin no more!"

Gradually, out of consideration for Betsey, I accepted her into our friendship.

One morning, while I was serving Goodwife Parris a little tea that her stomach tolerated better than gruel, she said softly: "Don't tell all those stories to the children. It makes them dream and dreaming isn't good for them."

I shrugged my shoulders. "Why shouldn't dreaming be good? Isn't it better than reality?"

She didn't answer and remained silent for a while. Then she went on: "Tituba, don't you think there's a curse on being a woman?"

I was annoyed. "Goodwife Parris, all you talk about is malediction. What is more beautiful than a woman's body! Especially when it is glorified by man's desire!"

"Be quiet! Be quiet!" she cried.

It was our only quarrel. In truth, I never understood its cause.

*   *   *

One morning we arrived in Boston.

I say it was morning, yet there was no indication from the light of day. A grayish mist fell from the sky and wrapped in its folds the forest of ships' masts, the piles of goods on the wharf, and the massive outline of the warehouses. An icy wind blew and both John Indian and I shivered in our cotton clothes. Despite their shawls Goodwife Parris and the children did the same. Only the master, like a ghost in the dirty, foggy light, kept his head up under his wide black-brimmed hat. We climbed down onto the wharf, John Indian stumbling under the weight of the luggage, while Samuel Parris condescended to let his wife lean on his arm. I took the little girls by the hand.

I could never have imagined that such a town as Boston existed, with its tall houses and crowds thronging the cobblestoned streets jammed with carts drawn by horse and oxen. I caught sight of a lot of faces the same color as mine and I understood that here too the children of Africa were paying their tribute to misfortune.

Samuel Parris seemed to know the place perfectly well, as not once did he stop to ask his way. At last we arrived, wet to the bone, in front of a two-story wooden house whose facade was enhanced by a crisscross of lighter beams. Samuel Parris let go of his wife's arm and said, as if it were the most remarkable of dwellings: "Here we are!"

The place smelled musty and damp. At the sound of our steps, two rats scampered off while a black cat that was dozing in the ash and dust rose lazily and sneaked off into the next room. I cannot describe the effect this unfortunate black cat had on the children, as well as on Elizabeth and Samuel. Samuel Parris seized his prayer book and began to recite a seemingly endless prayer. When he was a little calmer, he stood up straight and started to give orders: "Tituba, clean this room. Then prepare the beds. John Indian, come with me to buy some wood."

Once again John Indian put on the affected behavior that I hated so much. "Go outside, Master? In this wind and rain! You'll soon be spending money on wood for my coffin."

Without another word, Samuel Parris undid his large black cloth cape and threw it to him. Hardly had the two men gone out when Abigail asked, holding her breath: "Aunt, it was the devil, wasn't it?"

Elizabeth Parris's face convulsed. "Be quiet!"

"But what are you talking about?" I asked, intrigued.

"About the cat. The black cat."

"What will you think up next? It was only an animal that was disturbed by our arrival. Why do you keep talking about the devil? The invisible world around us only torments us if we provoke it. And surely this is not yet the case at your age."

"Liar!" hissed Abigail. "Poor, ignorant Negress. The devil

torments us all. We are all his victims. We shall all be damned, won't we, Aunt?"

When I saw the effect this conversation had on Goodwife Parris, and especially on poor Betsey, I quickly put an end to it. Whether it was the effect of this conversation or the cold that hung in the house despite the fire lit by John Indian, Goodwife Parris's health got worse that night. Samuel Parris came and woke me up about midnight. "I think she's about to go!"

No emotion in his voice. Merely an acknowledgment.

Die, my poor sweet Elizabeth? And leave the children alone with her monster of a husband? Die, my tormented lamb, without having learned that death is but a door through which the initiates come and go as they please? I jumped out of bed in my haste to be of help. But Samuel Parris stopped me. "Put your clothes on." Poor wretch, who at his wife's deathbed could think only of decency.

Up till then I had not called on the supernatural to care for Elizabeth Parris. I had merely kept her warm and had her swallow scalding hot drinks. The only liberty I had taken was to slip a little rum into her herb tea. That night I decided to use my powers. And yet I was lacking certain items required for practicing my art: the trees in which the invisible spirits repose, the condiments for their favorite dishes, and the plants and roots for healing.

What was I going to do in this unknown and inhospitable land across the sea? I decided to make substitutions. A maple tree whose foliage was turning red would do for a silk-cotton tree. Glossy, spiny holly leaves would replace the Guinea grass. Yellow, odorless flowers would do for the *salapertuis*, the panacea for all the body's ills, which only grows in the foothills back home. My prayers did the rest.

In the morning the color returned to Goodwife Parris's cheeks. She asked for a little water. Toward midday she managed to feed herself. And in the evening she went to sleep like a newborn babe. Three days later she gave me a smile as feeble as the sun through the gable window. "Thank you, Tituba! You saved my life!"

7

We stayed a year in Boston while Samuel Parris waited for his religious community, the Puritans, to offer him a parish. Alas! the offers did not exactly flow in! I believe that was because of Parris's personality. However fanatical and dour were those who shared his convictions, they were not as frightening as this tall, irate silhouette with his words of reprimand and warning. The little savings he had brought back from his incursion into the world of trade in Barbados melted like candle wax and we found ourselves in great difficulty. Sometimes all we had to eat for a whole day was dried apples. We had no firewood and we were chilled to the bone.

Then John Indian found a job in a tavern called the Black Horse. His job was to stoke the fires in the enormous fireplaces in front of which customers used to warm themselves, and to sweep up and empty any rubbish. He returned home at the first light of day, stinking of brandy and stout, but with leftovers hidden under his clothes. In a sleepy, drawling voice he would relate: "My angel, if you knew what was going on in this town of Boston, two doors away from these religious fanatics like our Samuel Parris, you wouldn't believe your eyes and ears. Whores, sailors with rings in their ears, ship's captains with greasy hair under their cocked hats, and even Bible-reading gentlemen with a wife and children at home. They all get drunk and swear and fornicate. Oh, Tituba, you can't imagine the hypocrisy of the white man's world."

I would put him to bed still chattering on.

Given his temperament, he soon made a lot of friends and he brought back their conversations. He told me that the slave trade was being intensified. Thousands of our people were being snatched from Africa. I learned that we were not the only ones the whites were reducing to slavery; they were also enslaving the Indians, the original inhabitants of both America and our beloved Barbados.

I listened in amazement and revulsion. "There are two Indians working at the Black Horse. If you could see how they are treated. They told me how they were deprived of their land, how the white man destroyed their herds and gave them 'fire water,' which sends a man to his grave in next to no time. Ah, white folks!"

These stories puzzled me and I tried to understand. "Perhaps it's because they have done so much harm to their fellow beings, to some because their skin is black, to others because their skin is red, that they have such a strong feeling of being damned?"

John was quite incapable of answering these questions, which, moreover, had never occurred to him. He was certainly the least miserable of any of us.

Although Samuel Parris of course never confided in me, it was easy to guess what he was thinking just from watching him locked up in his house like an animal in a cage, constantly praying or leafing through his formidable book. His constant presence affected us like a bitter potion. Gone were the secret, intimate conversations, the hurriedly told stories, gone were the songs quietly hummed. Instead he got it into his head to teach Betsey her letters and used a grisly alphabet:

A   In Adam's fall
    We sinnèd all.
B   Thy life to mend
    This Book attend.
C   The Cat doth play
    And after flay . . .

And so on. Poor Betsey, who was already so frail and impressionable, grew pale and trembled.

It was only from mid-April onward, when the weather cleared up, that Parris got into the habit of going out after lunch for a short walk. I took the opportunity to accompany the children into the small garden behind the house and then what games and gallopades we played! I removed the hideous hoods that made them look like old women, I undid their belts to get their blood circulating and to get their little bodies in a healthy sweat. Standing at the door, Elizabeth Parris would plead weakly: "Be careful, Tituba! Don't let them dance! Don't let them dance!" And yet the minute after she would contradict herself and be beating her hands in time, delighted with our dance steps.

I was allowed to take the girls to the Long Wharf, where we looked at the boats and the sea. Beyond this liquid expanse, a speck: Barbados.

How strange it is, this love of our own country. We carry it in us like our blood and vital organs. We only need to be separated from our native land to feel a pain that never loses its grip welling up inside us. I could see Darnell Davis's plantation, the arrogant Great House with its columns at the top of the hill, the black shack alleys seething with suffering and life, children with bloated stomachs, women wizened before their time, crippled men; and those cheerless surroundings I had lost suddenly meant so much that tears streamed down my cheeks.

The little girls, heedless of my mood, played in the puddles of dirty water, shoving each other and falling over among the ropes, and I couldn't help thinking of what Samuel Parris would say if he could witness such scenes. All their vitality, which was repressed day after day, hour after hour, surged out, and it was as if the Evil One they feared so much had at last taken possession of them. Of the two, Abigail was the more excitable, the more impetuous, and once again I marveled at her gift of dissimulation. As soon as we got back home, there she was dumb and rigid to the point of perfection in front of her uncle, repeating after him the words from the Holy Book. Were not her slightest gestures characterized by reserve and scruples of conscience? One afternoon, while we were coming back from Long Wharf, we witnessed a sight that left me with a terrible impression, never to be forgotten. As we came out of Front Street, the square—around which were grouped the prison, the courthouse, and the meeting house—was crowded with people. There was going to be an execution. The crowd was jostling around the foot of the raised platform where the gallows stood. A group of sinister men in wide-brimmed hats were busying themselves at its base. When we got closer we saw an old woman with a rope around her neck. Suddenly one of the men removed the plank on which she was standing and her body snapped stiff as a bow. There was a terrible cry and her head fell to one side.

I screamed and fell to my knees in the middle of this restless, inquisitive, almost joyful crowd.

It was as if I had been sentenced to relive my mother's execution. No, it wasn't an old woman hanging there. It was Abena in the flower of her youth and at the height of her beauty. Yes, it was she and I was six years old again. And my life had to begin all over again from that moment!

I screamed, and the more I screamed the more I felt the desire to scream. To scream out my suffering, my revolt, and my powerless rage. What kind of a world was this that had turned me into a slave, an orphan, and an outcast? What kind of a world that had taken me away from my own people? That had forced me to live among people who did not speak my language and who did not share my religion in their forbidding, unwelcoming land?

Betsey rushed up to me and clasped me in her tiny hands. "Be quiet! Oh, be quiet, Tituba!"

Abigail, who had been snooping around the crowd asking for bits of information, came back and said coldly: "Yes, be quiet! She only got what she deserved. She's a witch. She had bewitched the children of an honorable family."

I managed to get up and find our way back home. The whole town could talk of nothing but the execution. Those who had witnessed it told those who hadn't how Goody Glover had screamed when she saw death, like a dog howling at the moon, how her soul had escaped in the shape of a bat, while a nauseous pus, proof of her evildoing, seeped down her spindly legs. I hadn't seen anything of the sort. I had witnessed a sight of total barbarity.

It was shortly afterward that I realized I was pregnant and I decided to kill the child.

Apart from stolen kisses with Betsey and the secret sessions with Elizabeth Parris, the only moments of happiness in my sad existence were those I spent with John Indian.

Spattered with mud, shivering with cold, and worn out, my man made love to me every night. Since we slept in a cubby hole next to the Parris's bedroom we had to be careful not to utter any sighs or moans that might reveal the nature of our activities. Paradoxically, this merely heightened the passion of our lovemaking.

There is no happiness in motherhood for a slave. It is little more than the expulsion of an innocent baby, who will have no chance to change its fate, into a world of slavery and abjection. Throughout my childhood I had seen slaves kill their babies by sticking a long thorn into the still viscous-like egg of their heads, by cutting the umbilical cord with a poison blade, or else by abandoning them at night in a place frequented by angry spirits. Throughout my childhood I had heard slaves exchange formulas for potions, baths, and injections that sterilize the womb forever and turn it into a tomb lined with a scarlet shroud.

In Barbados, where I knew every plant by heart, I would have had no difficulty getting rid of an unwanted fruit. But what could I do here in Boston? Less than half a league outside Boston grew some thick forests that I decided to explore. One afternoon I managed to slip out, leaving Betsey in the clasp of her terrifying alphabet book and Abigail, her fingers busy with her needlework, but her mind clearly elsewhere, seated beside Goodwife Parris.

Once outside I realized to my surprise that these climes had a certain grace to them. The trees that had remained skeletal and sadly spindlelike for so long were now budding. Flowers dotted the meadows that stretched to infinity like a quiet, green sea.

As I was about to enter the forest, a man, a stiff, black silhouette on horseback, his face drowned in the shadow of his hat, called out to me: "Hey Negress! Aren't you afraid of the Indians?"

The Indians? I was less frightened of those "savages" than I was of the civilized beings I lived with who hanged old women from trees.

I was bending over a sweet-smelling bush that strongly resembled the many-virtued lemon grass when I heard someone
call my name. "Tituba!" I jumped. It was an old woman with
a face like a loaf of bread, shapeless yet pleasant enough.
"How do you know my name?" I asked in surprise.
She smiled mysteriously. "I knew you as a baby."
"Are you from Barbados?" I asked in growing amazement.
Her smile broadened. "Me? I've never left Boston. I arrived
with the Pilgrim Fathers and have never left them since. Well,
that's enough talk! If you stay out any longer Samuel Parris will
discover you've left the house and you'll have a lot of explaining
to do."
I didn't flinch. "I don't know you. What do you want of me?"
She began to trot into the forest, and as I didn't move, she
turned round and shouted: "Come on, don't be silly. I'm a
friend of Mama Yaya. My name is Judah White."

* * *

Old Judah told me the names and properties of each herb. I
made a mental note of some of the remedies whose secrets she
revealed to me:

To get rid of warts, rub them with a live toad until they are
finally drawn into the toad's skin.

In winter you can prevent scurvy by drinking tea made
from hemlock. (Be careful, the juice is deadly and can be
used for other purposes).

You will never have arthritis if you wear a ring made from
a raw potato on the middle finger of your left hand.

All wounds will heal much faster if you place cabbage
leaves on the affected area. For blisters, apply raw mashed
turnip.

For acute bronchitis, place the skin of a black cat on the
afflicted person's chest.

Toothache: chew tobacco leaves. Same for earache.

To treat diarrhea, drink tea made with blackberry leaves
three times a day.

I returned to Boston a little reassured, having learned to see friends in the black cat, the owl, the ladybird, and the mockingbird, creatures that I had never paid attention to previously. I turned Judah's words over in my head: "What would the world be like without us? Eh? What would it be like? Men hate us and yet without us their lives would be sad and narrow. Thanks to us they can change the present and sometimes read the future. Thanks to us they can hope. Tituba, we are the salt of the earth."

That night, my baby was carried out of my womb in a flow of black blood. I saw him wave his arms like a tadpole in distress and I burst into tears. John Indian also cried. I had not confided in him and he believed it to be another blow dealt by fate. It's true he was half drunk, having emptied numerous mugs of stout with the sailors who frequented the Black Horse tavern.

"My angel! There goes our solace for our old age! Who are we going to lean on when each of us is old and bent in this land without summer?"

I had trouble getting over the murder of my child. I knew that I had acted for the best. Yet the image of that little face whose actual features I would never know haunted me. By a strange aberration it seemed to me that the cry uttered by Goody Glover setting off along the corridor of death came from the bowels of my child, tortured by the same society and sentenced by the same judges.

Seeing my state of mind, Betsey and Elizabeth increased their attentions and kindnesses, which in other circumstances would not have failed to catch Samuel Parris's attention. But it so happened that he was constantly wrapped in an ever-growing gloom, since matters were going from bad to worse. The only money coming in was what John Indian earned stoking the fireplaces at the Black Horse. So we were literally dying of hunger. The children's faces grew thinner and their clothes became too large for them.

We were entering summer. The sun came and lit up the gray and blue roofs of Boston. It hung leaves on the branches of the trees. It planted long needles of fire in the sea. Despite the sadness of our lives, it made the blood throb in our veins.

A few weeks later Samuel Parris announced in a surly voice that he had accepted the offer of a parish and that we were leaving for the village of Salem, about twenty miles from Boston. John Indian, who always had the latest information, told me why Samuel Parris seemed less than enthusiastic. The village of Salem had a very bad reputation in the Bay Colony. On two occasions, two ministers, the Reverend James Bayley and the Reverend George Burroughs, had been hounded out of town by a large group of parishioners, who had refused to pay for their upkeep. The annual salary of sixty-six pounds was a pittance, especially as firewood was not included and the winters were severe in the forest. Finally, the Indians, wild barbarians who were set on scalping any head that came too close, lived all around Salem.

"Our master has not finished his studies."

"Studies?"

"Yes, theological studies to become a minister. And yet he expects to be treated like the Reverend Increase Mather or Cotton Mather himself."

"Who are they?"

John Indian grew bewildered. "I don't know, my lovely! I only hear their names being mentioned."

We spent a few more long weeks in Boston and I had time to note down Judah White's main recommendations:

Before moving into a house or immediately after having moved in, place a branch of mistletoe and some marjoram leaves at the corner of each room. Sweep the dust from west to east and burn it carefully before throwing the ashes outside. Sprinkle the floor with fresh urine, using your left hand.

At sunset burn twigs of *Populara indica* mixed with salt crystals.

Most important, prepare your garden and plant all the required medicinal herbs. Failing this, have them grow in earth-filled boxes. Don't forget to spit on them four times when waking.

I must confess that in many cases all this seemed very childish. In the West Indies our science is nobler and relies more on unseen forces than on things. But as Mama Yaya used to say: "When you get to the blind man's country, close both eyes."

8

Lament for my lost child

The moonstone dropped into the water,
Into the waters of the river,
And my fingers couldn't reach it,
Woe is me!
The moonstone has fallen.
Sitting on a rock on the riverbank
I wept and I lamented.
Oh, softly shining stone,
Glimmering at the bottom of the water.
The hunter passed that way
With his bow and arrows.
"Why are you crying, my lovely one?"
"I'm crying because my moonstone
Lies at the bottom of the water."
"If it is but that, my lovely,
I will help you."
But the hunter dived and was drowned.

I taught this lament to Betsey and we hummed it during the rare occasions when we were alone together. Her pretty little soft and melancholy voice harmonized perfectly with mine.

One day, to my surprise, I heard Abigail humming it too. I wanted to scold Betsey and tell her to keep the things I taught her to herself. Then once again I thought better of it. Wasn't Abigail her only playmate? And wasn't she but a child? A child could not be dangerous.

9

The village of Salem, in no way to be confused with the town of the same name, which I thought quite charming, was carved out of the forest like a bald spot in a mop of hair.

Samuel Parris had hired three horses and a cart and we were rather a sorry sight. Luckily, nobody came out to meet us. At that hour the men must have been in the fields, where the women brought them food and refreshment. Samuel Parris showed us the meeting house, an enormous building whose massive door was made of beams, and we continued on our way. How many inhabitants could Salem have? Surely, not more than two thousand, and coming from Boston the place seemed like a real hole. Cows wandered peacefully across the main street, jingling the bells around their necks, and I was surprised to see pieces of red cloth attached to their horns. The sickly smell of half a dozen pigs wallowing in a black mire rose up from an enclosure.

We arrived in front of the house that had been allotted to us. It stood a little askew in the middle of an immense garden completely overrun with weeds. Two black maples stood guard like candles and there was something repellent in the house's hostility. Samuel Parris helped down his poor wife, who had suffered greatly from the journey on horseback. I set my little Betsey on the ground, while Abigail jumped down and was about to run to the front door without waiting when Samuel Parris stopped her and thundered: "None of that, Abigail! Has the demon got into you?" Although I had little liking for Abigail, my heart missed a beat when I saw the effect this had on her.

The inside of the house reflected the outside: dark and hardly welcoming. However, a kind soul had lit a fire in each fireplace and the flames were gaily licking the firewood.

"How many bedrooms are there?" Elizabeth Parris asked. "Tituba, go and find those that are bright and sunny."

Samuel Parris had a reply to this as well, and crushing Elizabeth with one of his looks he let out: "The only room that is bright and sunny, is it not the coffin in the shadow of which each of us will one day lie?" Then he fell to his knees to thank the Lord for having protected us from wolves and other wild beasts that roam the forests between Boston and Salem. This prayer finally came to an end when the front door opened with a groan that made us all jump. A small woman, sadly attired in Puritan dress, but with a pleasant face, slipped into the room.

"I'm Goodwife Mary Sibley. I lit the fire for you. I also left a piece of beef, some carrots, turnips, and a dozen eggs in the kitchen for you."

Samuel Parris hardly said a word of thanks and continued the conversation: "Is it you, a woman, who is representing the congregation?"

Mary Sibley smiled. "The fourth commandment tells us to work by the sweat of our brow. The men are in the fields. As soon as they get back Deacon Ingersoll, Sergeant Thomas Putnam, Captain Walcott, and a few others will come to greet you."

Thereupon I went into the kitchen, thinking of the poor children's stomachs, in order to cook the piece of salted beef Goodwife Mary Sibley had been kind enough to bring. After a short while she came and joined me and stared me in the face.

"How come Samuel Parris has a nigger and a Negress in his service?"

She said it more out of naive curiosity than in spite. So I replied softly: "He's the one you should ask."

She remained silent for a moment, then concluded: "It's strange for a minister!" After a short while she thought of something else. "Elizabeth Parris is so pale! What is she suffering from?"

"Nobody knows exactly," I replied.

"I'm afraid this house won't do her any good." And she

lowered her voice. "Two women have already died in the bedroom upstairs. Mary Bayley, the wife of the first minister to this parish, and Judah Burroughs, the wife of the second."

In spite of myself, I let out a cry of alarm. For I knew full well how the dead who have not been laid to rest can trouble the living. Wouldn't I have to conduct a ceremony of purification and offer relief to these poor souls? Fortunately the house had a large garden, where I could come and go as I pleased. Mary Sibley followed the direction of my eyes and said in a troubled voice: "Ah yes, the cats. They're everywhere in Salem. We keep killing them off."

Hordes of cats were chasing each other in the grass, meowing and lying on their backs, nervously raising their paws that ended in sharp claws. A few weeks earlier I would have found nothing unnatural in such a sight. Now, instructed by Goodwife Judah White, I realized that the spirits of the place were greeting me. How childish white folks are to choose the cat as a manifestation of their powers! We others, we prefer animals of a nobler breed: the snake, for example, a magnificent reptile with dark rings.

As soon as I entered Salem, I knew I would not be happy there. I felt that I would undergo terrible trials and that excruciatingly painful events would turn my hair white.

When dusk fell, the men returned from the fields and the house filled with visitors. Anne Putnam and her husband, Thomas, a seven-foot giant, their daughter Anne, who immediately began to whisper in corners with Abigail, Sarah Houlton, John and Elizabeth Proctor, and so many others whose names I couldn't remember. I felt it was curiosity rather than kindness that brought them and they had come to judge and assess the minister in order to find out the role he would play in their village. Samuel Parris saw nothing suspect and behaved as he always did—despicably. He complained that no great piles of wood had been cut for his arrival and stacked in his barn. He complained that the house was decrepit, that the grass in the garden was knee-deep, and that the frogs made a din under his window.

Our move to Salem, however, was a cause for rejoicing, but

little did I know how fleeting this was to be. The house was so big that everybody could have his own room. John Indian and I could take refuge under the roof in a rather ugly attic whose ceiling was held up by a patchwork of worm-eaten beams. Here we could once again give rein to our unbridled love without fear of being heard.

In these uninhibited moments I could not help whispering: "John Indian, I'm afraid!"

He would caress my shoulder. "What will become of the world if our women are afraid? Things will fall apart! The heavens will collapse and the stars will roll in the dust! You afraid? Of what?"

"Of what tomorrow holds for us."

"Sleep, my princess! Tomorrow will be as radiant as a baby's smile."

The second piece of good fortune was that Samuel Parris was always out and about, taken up with the duties of his office. We hardly saw him at morning and evening prayers. When he was at home he was in bitter discussion with men about matters that did not sound religious.

"The sixty-six pounds of my salary come from contributions by the villagers and are in proportion to the area of their land."

"I must be supplied with firewood."

"On the Sabbath the contributions must be made in papers . . ." And so on. And behind his back life went on as usual.

* * *

I now had my kitchen full of little girls. I didn't like them all. I took a special dislike to Anne Putnam and the little servant girl, Mercy Lewis, who was about the same age and accompanied her everywhere. There was something in those two girls that made me have doubts about the innocence of childhood. Perhaps children cannot escape the frustrations and lasciviousness of adults after all. Whatever the case, Anne and Mercy reminded me constantly of Samuel Parris's speeches on Satan's presence in all of us. The same was true for Abigail. I sensed a violent streak in her, the power of her imagination to give a particular twist to the slightest everyday incident and this hatred—no, the word is not too strong—this hatred she had for the adult world, as if she could not forgive it for building a coffin around her youth.

Although I didn't like them all, I pitied them with their waxen skin and their bodies so full of promise yet mutilated like those trees that gardeners try to dwarf. In contrast, our childhood as little slaves, bitter though it was, seemed glowing, lit up by the joy of our games, our rambles, and our rovings together. We floated rafts made of sugarcane on the rushing streams. We grilled pink and yellow fish on little crisscrosses of green wood. We danced. And it was this pity of mine, against which I was helpless, that made me tolerate these children around me and encouraged me to entertain them. I wouldn't stop until I had managed to get one of them to burst out laughing and plead: "Tituba! Oh, Tituba!"

Their favorite stories were about people in league with the devil. They sat in a circle around me and I could smell the sharp scent of their sparingly washed bodies. They assailed me with questions.

"Tituba, do you think there are people in league with the devil living in Salem?"

I nodded and laughed. "Yes, I think Sarah Good must be one." Sarah Good was still a young woman, but she was hunched over and a beggar. The children were afraid of her because of the stinking pipe she always had stuck between her teeth and because of her constant muttering. It seemed as if she was mumbling prayers that nobody could understand except herself. Apart from that, she was a generous soul, at least I thought so.

"Do you think so, Tituba?" the children cheeped. "And Sarah Osborne, is she one too?"

Sarah Osborne was an old woman, not a beggar like the other Sarah, but well-off, the owner of a lovely oak-paneled house, who in her youth had committed some fault or other to her discredit.

I took a deep breath and pretended to think hard, letting them stew in their curiosity, before solemnly declaring: "Perhaps!"

Abigail insisted. "Have you seen them both fly with their

skin all scorched? And Elizabeth Proctor, have you seen her? Have you?"

Mistress Proctor was one of the nicest women in the village, the only one who was kind enough to talk to me about slavery, about the country I came from and its inhabitants.

"You know very well, Abigail, that I'm joking," I said severely. And I sent everyone away.

When I was left alone with Betsey she, too, asked me in her high-pitched voice: "Do people in league with the devil actually exist, Tituba? Do they?"

I took her in my arms. "What does it matter? Aren't I here to protect you if they try to harm you?"

She looked straight at me and a shadow that I tried to dispel was dancing at the back of her eyes.

"Tituba knows the words that cure every sickness, that heal every wound, and untie every knot. Don't you know that?"

She remained silent, her body trembling even more despite my words of consolation. I hugged her up against me and the wings of her heart beat desperately like a bird in a cage, while I said over and over again: "Tituba can do anything. Tituba knows everything. Tituba sees everything."

Soon the circle of little girls got bigger. At Abigail's instigation a string of great gawks whose breasts filled out their pinafores and whose blood, I'm sure, reddened their thighs occasionally, thronged into my kitchen. I didn't like them at all. Neither Mary Walcott nor Elizabeth Booth nor Susanna Sheldon. Their eyes conveyed all the contempt of their parents for those of our race. And yet they needed me to season the insipid gruel of their lives. So instead of asking me, they ordered me: "Tituba, sing us a song!" "Tituba, tell us a story! No, we don't want that one. Tell us the one about the people in league with the devil."

One day things turned sour. Fat Mary Walcott was hovering around me and finally said: "Tituba, is it true you know everything, you see everything and can do everything? You're a witch then?"

I lost my temper. "Don't use words whose meaning you don't know. Do you know what a witch really is?"

"Of course we do," intervened Anne Putnam. "It's someone who has made a pact with the devil. Mary's right. Are you a witch, Tituba? I think you must be."

This was too much. I drove all these young vipers out of my kitchen and chased them into the street. "I never want to see you around here again. Never!"

When they had scattered, I took little Betsey and scolded her: "Why do you repeat everything I tell you? You see how they change the meaning?"

The child turned scarlet and curled up against me. "Forgive me, Tituba. I won't tell them anything again."

Betsey had changed since we had come to Salem. She was becoming nervous and irritable, always crying for nothing at all or staring off into space with her eyes as big as halfpennies.

I became worried. Were the spirits of the two people who had died upstairs in unknown circumstances influencing her fragile nature? Did the child need protection like her mother?

There was nothing pleasant in my new life. From day to day my apprehensions grew stronger and heavier, like a burden I could never put down. I slept with it. It hung over me above John Indian's muscular body. In the morning it made me drag my feet on the stairs and gripped my hands while I was preparing the tasteless gruel for breakfast.

I was no longer myself. To try and console myself I used a remedy. I filled a bowl with water, which I placed near the window so that I could look at it while I busied myself in the kitchen and imagine my Barbados. The bowl of water managed to encompass the entire island, with the swell of the sea merging into the waves of the sugarcane fields, the leaning coconut palms on the seashore, and the almond trees loaded with red and dark green fruit. Although I had trouble making out the inhabitants, I could see the hills clearly, the cabins, the sugar mills, and the ox carts whipped on by invisible hands. I got a glimpse of the Great Houses and the masters' graveyards. And all that moved silently at the bottom of my bowl of water. Yet this presence heartened me. Sometimes Abigail, Betsey, and Mistress Parris caught me in contemplation and would ask in surprise: "What are you looking at, Tituba?"

I was tempted many times to share my secret with Betsey

and Goodwife Parris, who I knew yearned for Barbados. But each time I thought otherwise, moved by a newly acquired vigilance, dictated to me by my environment. And then I would ask myself, how could their yearning and nostalgia possibly be compared to mine? What they yearned for was the sweetness of a gentler life, the life of white women who were served and waited on by attentive slaves. Even if the Reverend Mr. Parris had ended up losing all his wealth and hopes, the life they had spent there was composed of luxury and voluptuousness. And what did I yearn for? The subtle joys of being a slave. The cakes made out of crumbs from the stale bread of life. The fleeting moments of forbidden games.

We did not belong to the same universe, Goodwife Parris, Betsey, and I, and all the affection in the world could not change that.

When in early December Betsey's absences of mind and carelessness overstepped the bounds (she could not even recite their creed and understandably received a beating from Samuel Parris), I decided to give her a magic bath.

I made her swear not to tell anyone and at dusk I plunged her up to her neck in a liquid to which I had given all the properties of amniotic fluid. I had needed no less than four working days under the difficult conditions of exile to obtain them. But I was proud of the results. Plunging Betsey into this scalding hot bath, it seemed to me that these same hands, that not long ago had dealt death were now giving life, and I was purifying myself of the murder of my child. I had her repeat the ritual words before ducking her head under water, then suddenly bringing her back up choking, her eyes full of tears. After that, I wrapped her scarlet body in a large blanket and took her back to bed. She slept like a log, in a deep, undisturbed sleep; something she had not done on many previous nights when she would call out in her pleading little voice: "Tituba! Tituba! Please come!"

Shortly before midnight, when I was sure not to meet a soul in the streets, I went out to throw away the water from the magic bath at a crossroads. That's what I had always been told to do.

How the night changes from one country to another. Night

on our island is a womb that renders you atremble and powerless again, but paradoxically unleashes the senses that catch the slightest whisper of things and human beings. In Salem night was a black wall of hostility that I was constantly walking into. Animals, crouched in the dark trees, screeched evilly as I went by, while a thousand malevolent eyes stared after me. I passed the familiar shape of a black cat. Strangely, instead of greeting me with the customary words of consolation, this one meowed angrily and arched its back under the moon.

I walked at a brisk pace to the Dobbin crossroads. There I set down the pail I had balanced on my head and slowly but surely spread its contents on the ground white with frost. When the last drop had soaked into the earth, I heard a rustle in the grass. I knew that Mama Yaya and Abena, my mother, were not far away. But once again they did not appear and I merely sensed their silent presence.

Soon winter completed its circle around Salem. The snow piled up to the window ledges and every morning I battled against it with buckets of hot water and salt. Whatever I did, however, it always had the last word. Soon the sun no longer deigned to rise and the days dragged on in dark foreboding.

10

I had not realized the full extent of the ravages that Samuel Parris's religion was causing nor even understood its real nature before coming to live in Salem. Imagine a small community of men and women oppressed by the presence of Satan and seeking to hunt him down in all his manifestations. A cow that died, a child smitten with convulsions, a girl whose menstrual period was late in coming set off a chain of unending speculation. Who had caused such catastrophes by driving a bargain with the formidable enemy? Wasn't it the fault of Bridget Bishop, who hadn't been to the meeting house two Sundays in a row? No, wasn't it rather Giles Cory, who had been seen feeding a stray animal on the afternoon of the Sabbath? Even I was being poisoned in this putrifying atmosphere and I caught myself reciting incantations and performing ritual gestures at the slightest occasion. What is more, I had very precise reasons for being worried. In Bridgetown Susanna Endicott had already told me she was convinced my color was indicative of my close connections with Satan. I was able to laugh that off, however, as the ramblings of a shrew embittered by solitude and approaching old age. In Salem such a conviction was shared by all.

There were two or three black servants in the community, how they got there I have no idea, and all of us were not simply cursed, but visible messengers of Satan. So we were furtively approached to try and assuage unspeakable desires for revenge, to liberate unsuspecting hatred and bitterness, and to do evil by every means. He who passed for the most devoted of husbands dreamed of nothing but killing his wife! She who passed for the most faithful of wives was prepared to sell the soul of her children to get rid of the father! Neighbor wanted to exterminate neighbor, a brother, his sister. Even the children themselves wanted to be rid of one or the other of their parents in the most painful way possible. And it was the putrid smell of all these crimes seeking to be committed that turned me into another woman. And in vain did I stare at the blue waters of my bowl, thinking of the banks of the River Ormond. Something inside me was slowly but surely coming undone.

Yes, I was becoming another woman. A stranger to myself. One set of circumstances completed the transformation. No doubt hard-pressed for money and unable to purchase a horse, Samuel Parris hired John Indian out to Deacon Ingersoll to help him with the field work. John Indian, therefore, only came home to sleep with me on Saturdays, the day before the Sabbath, when God orders even the niggers to rest. Night after night then I curled myself up into a ball under a threadbare blanket in a room without a fire, panting with desire for my absent husband. Very often when John Indian came back to me he was so exhausted from having labored like a beast that, despite his robust physique that up till then had satisfied my desires, he fell asleep almost as soon as his head touched my breast. I stroked his rough, curly hair, filled with pity and revolt against our fate. Who, who had created this world?

In my helplessness and despair I started to think about revenge. But how? I devised schemes that I would reject at dawn, only to start reconsidering them at dusk. I lost my appetite. I could hardly drink. I wandered like a lost soul wrapped in my coarse woolen shawl, followed by one or two black cats, no doubt sent by Goody Judah White to remind me that I was not quite alone. Not surprising that the villagers of Salem stood aghast at me, I looked so awesome!

Awesome and hideous. My uncombed hair formed a mane around my head. My cheeks became hollow and my mouth pouted brazenly, stretched to the limits over my swollen gums.

When John Indian was with me, he gently complained: "You're neglecting yourself, wife. You used to be a meadow where I grazed. Now the tall grass of your pubis and the tufts of your armpits almost disgust me."

"Forgive me, John Indian, and continue to love me even if I am worthless."

Black Witch of Salem

I got in the habit of roaming through the forest, because tiring out my body seemed to tire my mind as well and therefore I could get a little sleep. The snow whitened the footpaths and the trees looked like skeletons with their gnarled branches.

One day, upon entering a clearing, I had the impression of approaching a prison whose marble walls were closing in on me. I could see the white mottled sky through a tiny opening above my head and I believed my life was going to end there, wrapped in a glistening shroud. Would my soul find its way back to Barbados? And even if it did, would it be condemned to wander helplessly, without a voice, like Mama Yaya and Abena, my mother? I recalled their words: "You'll be so far away and it will take so much time to cross the water!" Ah, I should have plied them with questions! I should have forced them to break the rules and tell me what I couldn't guess! For one thought came back time and time again: if my body followed the law of nature, would my soul, once delivered, set off back to my native land? I'm reaching the land I lost. I'm returning to the forsaken hideousness of its sores. I recognize it by its smell. The smell of sweat, suffering, and labor. But paradoxically a warm, strong smell that reassures me.

Once or twice while wandering through the forest I met some of the villagers bending awkwardly over herbs and plants, their deceitful faces revealing the schemes in their hearts. I got great amusement from this. The art of doing evil is a complex one. If it is based on the knowledge of plants, this must be combined with the power to act on the unseen forces, which are rebellious by nature, transient as air, and need to be invoked. Not just anyone can set herself up as a witch!

One day while I was sitting on the ground that sparkled with frost, hugging the folds of my skirt around me, I saw the darting, familiar silhouette of little Sarah, Joseph Henderson's black slave, emerge from between the trees. On seeing me she started to run off, then changed her mind and came closer. I have already said there were several blacks in Salem who were made to work their fingers to the bone and were treated worse than the animals they were often in charge of.

Joseph Henderson, who came from Rowley, had married one

68

I, Tituba

of the Putnam daughters, the richest family in the village. Perhaps the marriage had been planned by Joseph Henderson for financial advantage. In any case, it hadn't paid off. For various sordid reasons the couple had not received the land they had hoped for and they were now destitute. Perhaps this was why Goodwife Priscilla Henderson was always the first to enter the meeting house, the first to sing out the prayers, and the one most set on beating her servant. Nobody was surprised any longer at the welts that adorned Sarah's face or at the strong smell of garlic with which she tried to treat them.

She dropped down beside me and blurted out: "Tituba, help me!"

I took her tiny hand, rough and rigid like a badly planed piece of wood, and asked: "How can I help you?"

Her eyes flickered. "Everyone knows you have magical skills. Help me to get rid of her."

I remained silent for a moment, and then shook my head. "I cannot do what your heart dares not disclose. The woman who revealed to me her science taught me to heal and console rather than to do evil. Once, when, like yourself, I dreamed of doing my worst, she warned: 'Don't become like them, knowing only how to do evil.'"

She shrugged her frail shoulders under her wretched shawl. "Knowledge must adapt itself to society. You are no longer in Barbados among our unfortunate brothers and sisters. You are among monsters who are set on destroying us."

On hearing this, I wondered whether it was really little Sarah speaking or whether it was not my innermost thoughts that were echoing in the forest. To avenge myself. To avenge ourselves. Me, John Indian, Mary Black, Sarah, and all the others. Unleash the fire and the storm. Dye scarlet the white shroud of snow.

"Don't talk like that, Sarah!" I said in a troubled voice. "Come and see me in my kitchen. There are plenty of dried apples if you are hungry."

She got up and the contempt in her eyes burned me like acid. I walked slowly back to the village. Wasn't Sarah conveying to me some message from the invisible world and hadn't I better spend three nights in prayer, calling to the spirits with all my strength: "Cross the waters, O my fathers, Cross the waters, O my mothers, I'm so alone in this distant land! Cross the waters"!

Deep in thought, I was passing Goodwife Rebecca Nurse's house when I heard someone call my name. Goodwife Rebecca Nurse was almost seventy-one and I had never seen anyone so crippled with pain. Sometimes her legs swelled up so much that she couldn't move an inch and she remained stranded in her bed like one of those whales you see from the slave ships. More than once her children had called me to her and I had always managed to provide relief. On that day I thought her old face looked less drawn and she smiled at me. "Give me your arm, Tituba, so that I can walk a few steps with you."

I obeyed and we walked down the street that led to the center of the village, still lit by a pale sun. Once again I was deep in thought about my terrible dilemma when I heard Rebecca Nurse murmur: "Tituba, can't you punish them? It's those Houltons again who forgot to tie up their hogs and they've ruined our vegetable garden once more . . ."

For a moment I didn't understand. Then I realized what she expected of me. I was seized with anger and let go her arm, leaving her all askew in front of a fence.

Oh no, they won't get me to be the same as they are! I will not give in. I will not do evil!

＊ ＊ ＊

A few days later Betsey fell ill.

I was not surprised. I had somewhat neglected her during recent weeks, so taken up was I with my own problems and state of mind. I can't even remember whether I said a prayer for her in the morning and had her swallow a potion. To tell the truth, I hardly saw her. She spent most of her time with Anne Putnam, Mercy Lewis, Mary Walcott, and the others who, now barred from my kitchen, locked themselves upstairs and indulged in all sorts of games of a dubious nature.

One day Abigail showed me a set of tarot cards that she had found somewhere and asked: "Do you think we can read the future with these?"

I shrugged my shoulders. "Abigail, my dear, those little bits of colored cardboard would hardly suffice."

She then brandished her very pale, curved palm, where the lines of her hand were traced out.

"And there, do you think you can read the future there?"

I shrugged my shoulders and didn't answer. Yes, I knew that the group of girls was playing dangerous games. But I closed my eyes. Wasn't all this foolishness, this whispering and giggling their revenge on their awful humdrum existence?

> "In Adam's fall,
> We sinnèd all. . . ."

> "Sin is on our forehead,
> We cannot wipe it out."

And so on.

At least for a few hours they became light and carefree.

Then one evening after supper, Betsey dropped rigid to the ground and remained with her arms spread out, her eyes bulging, and her mouth gaping over her milk teeth. I rushed to help her, but hardly had my hand touched her arm than she recoiled and uttered a scream. I remained speechless. Goodwife Parris quickly picked her up in her arms and even went so far as to shower her with kisses.

I went back to my kitchen.

When night had fallen and everyone had retired to their bedchambers I waited cautiously a few moments and then stole down the wooden stairs. Holding my breath, I peeped into Betsey's room, but to my surprise it was empty, as if her parents had taken her with them to protect her from some unknown evil.

I could not help recalling the look that Goodwife Parris had given me. The unknown evil that had struck Betsey could only have come from me. A mother's ingratitude!

Ever since we had left Bridgetown, my devotion to Goodwife Parris and Betsey had been unceasing. I had watched for the slightest sneeze and stopped their first bouts of coughing. I had seasoned their gruel and put spices in their broth. I had gone out in the wind to look for a pound of treacle and braved the snow for a few kernels of corn.

Now, in the twinkling of an eye, all that had been forgotten and I had become the enemy. Perhaps, in fact, I had never ceased to be one and Goodwife Parris was jealous of the ties I had with her daughter.

If I had been less distressed, I would have endeavored to reason and to understand this about-face. Elizabeth Parris had been living for months in the rotting atmosphere of Salem with people who took me for Satan's deputy and didn't mind saying so, surprised that I was allowed to live with John Indian in a Christian household. It is likely that such remarks could have corrupted her in turn, even if at first she had strongly resisted them. But with the pain I felt, I was quite incapable of keeping a proper perspective. In a state of mental torture I went up to my room and went to bed with my solitude and grief. The night dragged on.

The next morning I came down as usual to prepare breakfast. There were some lovely fresh eggs and I was whipping them up to make an omelet when I heard the family take their seats around the table for morning prayers. "Tituba!" Samuel Parris boomed.

This is how he called me each morning, but this morning there was a particular menace in his voice. I went in slowly. Hardly had I appeared in the doorway with the ends of my shawl tied around me, for the fire had only just been lit and was not yet giving off any heat, than my little Betsey jumped from her chair and began to scream, writhing on the ground.

Her screams were not human.

Every year the slaves used to fatten a pig that they killed two days before Christmas Eve so that the meat could marinate in lemon and bay-rum leaves to rid it of any impurities. They would slit the animal's throat at dawn, then hang it up by its feet from the branches of a calabash tree. While its blood flowed out, at first in great gushes, then slowing to a trickle, it screamed. Unbearable, jarring screams, suddenly silenced by death.

That's how Betsey was screaming. As if suddenly this child's body had been changed into a vile animal inhabited by monstrous forces.

Abigail at first remained standing, clearly aghast. Then, missing nothing, she looked from the accusing eyes of Samuel Parris to the hardly less terrifying face of Goodwife Parris, and on to mine, which must have expressed total distress. She seemed to understand what was going on and consequently, as if boldly plunging into a pond without knowing what lay beneath the greenish surface, she jumped off her seat and started to scream, writhing on the floor in the same way.

This hideous concert lasted a few minutes. After that, the two children seemed to fall into catalepsy.

"Tituba, what have you done to them?" Samuel Parris asked.

If I could, I would have rebuffed him with a tremendous burst of laughter and then gone back to my kitchen. Instead, I remained nailed to the spot in terror, staring at the two girls without being able to utter a word. Finally, Goodwife Parris exclaimed in a whining voice: "You see what your spells have done!"

"Goodwife Parris," I retorted quickly, "when you were sick, who looked after you? In the hovel in Boston, where you almost died, who brought out the sun and cured you? Wasn't it me? But I didn't hear any talk about spells then."

Samuel Parris spun round like a wild animal that has found another prey and thundered: "Elizabeth Parris, speak out! You too indulged in these games with Satan?"

The poor creature tottered and fell to her knees at the feet of her husband. "Forgive me, Samuel Parris, for I knew not what I was doing!"

I had no idea what Samuel Parris would have done if at that moment Betsey and Abigail had not come out of their trance and started screaming even harder, as if they were damned.

Our neighbors, aroused by the din, soon started hammering on the front door. Samuel Parris's face changed in a flash. Placing a finger to his lips, he grabbed hold of the two children and took them upstairs, along with some firewood. After a moment Goodwife Parris composed herself and opened the door, stammering reassuringly: "It's nothing, nothing at all. The Reverend Parris has decided to give his daughters a beating this morning."

The newcomers noisily agreed. "Should be done more often, if you ask me."

Goodwife Sheldon, whose daughter Susanna shut herself up daily with Abigail, uttered the first note of discord. "It sounds like the Goodwin children. I hope they haven't been bewitched!"

As she spoke, she of course stared at me with her pale, cruel eyes.

Goodwife Parris managed to drag out a ripple of laughter. "What are you thinking of, Goodwife Sheldon? Don't you know that a child is like bread that requires kneading? And believe me, Samuel Parris is an excellent baker!"

Everybody guffawed.

I went back to my kitchen. After thinking the matter over, things became clear. Voluntarily or involuntarily, consciously or unconsciously, something or someone had turned Betsey against me, for I truly believed that Abigail was but an accomplice in the matter, skillful at playing the game to her advantage. I had to regain the child's confidence, which I felt I could surely do if I could be alone with her.

I then needed to protect myself, which I had neglected to do. I had to render a blow for a blow. An eye for an eye. Mama Yaya's old humanitarian lessons were no longer valid. Those around me were as ferocious as the wolves that howled at the moon in the forests outside Boston and I had to become as ferocious as they were.

There was one thing, however, that I didn't know: evil is a gift received at birth. There's no acquiring it. Those of us who have not come into this world armed with spurs and fangs are losers in every combat.

"I have been watching you, my poor suffering wife, during all these years we have been together and I can see that you don't understand this white man's world in which we live. You make exceptions. You believe that some of them can respect and love us. How mistaken you are! You must hate without distinction!"

"Well, you're a fine one to talk, John Indian! You're like a puppet in their hands. I'll pull this string and you pull that one . . ."

"I wear a mask, my tormented wife. Painted the colors they want. Red, bulging eyes? 'Yes, Massa!' Thick, black lips? 'Yes Missy!' The nose flattened like a toad? 'At your service, ladies and gentlemen!' And behind all that, I, John Indian, am free. I watched you lick that little Betsey like barley sugar and I say to myself: 'I just hope she ain't going to be disappointed!' "

"You think she didn't love me then?"

"We're niggers, Tituba. The whole world's working against us."

I curled up against John Indian, for his words were too cruel. Finally I stammered: "What's going to happen now?"

He thought for a moment. "Samuel Parris is as anxious as anyone not to let the rumor out in Salem that his daughters have been bewitched. He'll have Dr. Griggs come in and hope it's just a commonplace illness. Things will only go wrong if the unfortunate doctor can't cure them!"

"John Indian," I groaned, "Betsey can't be sick. I protected her from everything."

"And that's the unfortunate part about it," he interrupted. "You wanted to protect her. She told everything in detail, oh, quite innocently I'm sure, to Abigail and her set of little bitches, who turned it into poison. Alas, she was the first to be poisoned."

I burst into tears. John Indian had no words of consolation for me. Instead, he said in a rough voice: "Remember, you're Abena's daughter."

This brought me back to myself.

The daylight filtered in, as dirty as a rag, through the narrow skylight. We had to get up and go about our daily chores.

Samuel Parris was already up and preparing to go to the meeting house, as it was Sabbath day. His black hat was pulled down low over his forehead, reducing his face to a rigid triangle. He turned toward me. "Tituba, I do not accuse without evidence. So I shall reserve my judgment. But if tomorrow Dr. Griggs sees the influence of Satan, I shall show you the man I am."

"What do you call evidence?" I scoffed.

He continued to stare at me. "I'll have you confess what you did to my children and I'll have you hanged by the neck. What a magnificent fruit swinging from the trees of Massachusetts."

At that moment Goodwife Parris and the two girls entered the room; Abigail was holding the prayer book.

She was the first to go down and start screaming. Betsey remained standing for a moment, her face scarlet, hesitating, it seemed to me, between affection and terror. Then she fell down beside Abigail.

I screamed in turn: "Stop it, stop it! You know full well, Betsey and Abigail, that I never did you any harm. Especially you, Betsey. Everything I did was for your good."

Samuel Parris marched up to me and I staggered under the wave of his hatred as if I had been struck.

"Explain yourself! You've said one word too many. What did you do to them?"

Once again I was saved by a crowd of neighbors who, like the day before, had come to see what all the noise was about. They formed a circle in respect and silent horror around the children, who continued to be afflicted by the most indecent convulsions. John Indian, who had also come down without saying a word, went to fetch a bucket of water from the kitchen and whoosh! threw it over our little devils. This calmed them down. They got up, streaming with water, almost apologetic, and we set off in a procession to the meeting house.

The commotion started up again while we were taking our seats in our pews. John Indian usually went first and I next, so that the children could sit between me and Goodwife Parris. When it was Abigail's turn to come and kneel beside me, she stopped, leaped backward into the aisle, and began to scream.

And at the Sunday service in Salem, can you imagine! They were all there, John Putnam, the rum merchant; Thomas Putnam, the sergeant, and his wife, Anne; Giles Corey and his wife, Martha; their daughters and their daughters' husbands; Johanna Chibum; Nathaniel Ingersoll; John and Elizabeth Proctor; and all the rest. I also recognized Abigail's and Betsey's companions in their dangerous games, those young girls whose eyes were shining with excitement. They were dying to roll on the ground too and to attract everybody's attention. I felt that at any moment they would fall into a trance as well.

This time it was only Abigail who went into a fit and made a fuss. Betsey did not follow suit. So after a while Abigail shut up and remained prostrate with her hair straggling out of her hood. John Indian stood up, stepped out of the pew, took her in his arms, and went home. The rest of the service went by without incident.

*　*　*

I confess that I am naive. I was convinced that even a race of villains and criminals could produce some good, well-meaning individuals, just as a stunted tree can bear some healthy fruit. I believed in the affection of Betsey, led astray by some unknown force, but I was sure of winning her back. When Goodwife Parris went down to meet the crowd of curious neighbors who had come for news of the children, I took that opportunity to go up to Betsey's room.

She was sitting against the window, her fingers resting on her needlework, and in the half light her little face was so expressive that my heart went out to her. On hearing me come in, she looked up and immediately rounded her mouth to let out a shriek. I rushed over to her and placed my hand over her mouth.

She bit me so hard she drew blood and we remained looking at each other while a red pool began to form on the floor.

Despite the pain, I asked as quietly as I could: "Betsey, who has turned you against me?"

She shook her head. "Nobody, nobody."

"Is it Abigail?" I insisted.

She continued to shake her head more and more nervously. "No, no, they only said that what you were doing to me was evil."

I went on in the same tone of voice. "Why do you tell them about it? Didn't I say it was to remain a secret between us two?"

"I couldn't, I couldn't! All those things you did to me."

"Didn't I say it was for your own good?"

Her upper lip curled up into an ugly pout, revealing her sick gums. "You, do good? You're a Negress, Tituba! You can only do evil. You are evil itself."

I had already heard these words or else read them in what people were thinking. But I never imagined they would come from the lips of someone so dear to me. I remained speechless. Betsey hissed like a green mamba from the islands: "That bath you had me take; what was in it? The blood of a newborn baby that died from one of your spells?"

I was aghast.

"That cat you feed every morning; that's Him, isn't it?"

I started to cry.

"When you went out into the forest it was to meet the others like yourself, and dance with them, wasn't it?"

I managed to drag myself out of the room. I crossed the dining room full of chattering, excited matrons and withdrew into my kitchen. Someone had removed the bowl in which I gazed on my Barbados and I sat down on a stool, heavy with grief. While I was there, huddled over myself, Mary Sibley came to look for me. I had no more liking for her than for the rest of the women in the village. Yet I must confess that once or twice she had talked to me with a fair amount of compassion about the fate dealt out to blacks by white folks.

She took me by the arm. "Listen Tituba. Soon the pack of wolves will be on you, will be tearing you to pieces and licking their lips before the blood curdles and loses its taste. You must stand up for yourself and prove that these children have not been bewitched."

This took me by surprise and, mistrustful of this unexpected attention, I said: "I would like to very much. But unfortunately I don't know how."

She lowered her voice. "You're the only one who doesn't. All you have to do is to make them a cake. But instead of kneading it with flour and water you mix in a little urine. Then once it is baked in the oven, it's ready to eat."

"Goodwife Sibley," I interrupted, "with all due respect, go and tell your old wives' tales to someone else!"

She spun round to John Indian, who came in at that moment. "Does she know, does she know what they do to witches? I'm trying to help her and all she does is laugh in my face."

John Indian began to roll his eyes from left to right and in a tearful voice said: "Oh, please, Goodwife Sibley, help us! Help poor Tituba and poor John Indian!"

But I did not move an inch. "Go and tell your old wives' tales to someone else, Goodwife Sibley!"

She went out, most offended, followed by John Indian, who was trying in vain to calm her down. At the end of the afternoon, the very same girls I had driven out of my kitchen came in one after the other. Not one was missing. Anne Putnam, Mary Walcott, Elizabeth Hubbard, Mary Warren, Mercy Lewis, Elizabeth Booth, Susanna Sheldon, and Sarah Churchill. And it was clear they had come to tease me. They had come to wallow in the sight of my ruin. Oh, this was still only the beginning! I would fall much farther. I would get hurt much more. And with this happy thought, their eyes gleamed with cruelty. They had turned almost lovely in their shapeless dresses! They had become almost desirable: Mary Walcott with her buttocks as big as a trunk, Mary Warren with her breasts like two shrivelled pears, and Elizabeth Hubbard with her teeth sticking out of her mouth like millstones.

* * *

That night I dreamed of Susanna Endicott and I remembered her words: "Alive or dead, I shall haunt you."

Was this then her revenge? Was she dead and buried in the graveyard at Bridgetown? Had her house been sold to the highest bidder and her money been distributed to the poor, as she had wanted?

Was this then her revenge?

John Indian had gone back to work for Deacon Ingersoll and my bed was as cold and empty as the grave that some were digging for me. I drew open the curtain and saw the moon sitting sidesaddle in the sky. A scarf of clouds was knotted around her neck and the sky behind was the color of ink.

I shivered and went back to bed.

Shortly before midnight my door opened and I was in such a state of nervousness and affliction that I sat up with a jump. It was Samuel Parris. He didn't say a word and remained standing in the shadows, mumbling some prayer or other. I could not say how long his tall silhouette remained immobile against the wall. Then he left as silently as he had come and I could make believe it was all a dream. He, too, was a dream.

By morning, sleep had taken me into his loving arms. He was considerate with me. He took me on a walk across the hills of Barbados. I saw the cabin where I had spent so many happy days in solitude, which I now realized had been the best of all possible worlds. My cabin hadn't changed a bit. Just a little more rickety. Just a little more mossy. The trellis was laden with passion fruit. The calabash tree was showing swellings like the womb of a pregnant woman. The River Ormond was gurgling like a newborn baby.

Will I ever find my way back to you, my lost, beloved country?

Dr. Griggs and I were on excellent terms. He knew that I had done wonders for Goodwife Parris's languishing fits and that it was thanks to me she could sing the Sunday psalms at the meeting house. He also knew that I had cured the girls' coughs and bronchitis. Once he had even come to ask me for a poultice to treat a bad wound his son had had on his ankle. Up till then he seemed to find no malice in my art. But that morning when he pushed open the door to Samuel Parris's house, his eyes avoided mine and I realized he was about to join the side of the accusers. He went up the stairs to the second floor and on the landing I heard him consult in a muffled voice with the minister and Goodwife Parris. After a while, Samuel Parris's voice boomed out: "Tituba, you'll have to be present."

I obeyed.

Betsey and Abigail were in their parents' bedchamber, sitting on either side of the huge bed that was covered with an eiderdown. I no sooner entered than they dropped to the ground in harmony, uttering shrieks at the top of their voices. Dr. Griggs did not let this put him off. He laid on the table a number of big, leather-bound books, which he opened at carefully numbered pages and began to read with the utmost seriousness. Then he turned to Goodwife Parris and ordered her to undress the two girls. The unfortunate woman seemed scared out of her wits and I remembered our secret conversation about her husband: "My poor Tituba, he lies with me without taking off either his clothes or mine." These people could not bear nudity, not even a child's. Dr. Griggs repeated in a voice that would clearly not tolerate any further hesitation or contradiction: "Undress them!"

She had to obey. I won't linger over the difficulty she had in undressing the girls, who writhed about like a worm cut in two and screamed as if they were being skinned alive. She managed, however, to finish the job and the girls' bodies emerged, Betsey's perfectly childlike, Abigail's nearing adolescence with her ugly tuft of pubic hair and the rosy rounds of her nipples. Dr. Griggs examined them carefully despite the abominable curses Abigail showered him with, since she had begun to pepper her screams with the vilest of insults.

Finally he turned to Samuel Parris and solemnly declared: "I can see no disorder of the spleen or the liver nor congestion of the bile or overheating of the blood. In a word, I can see no physical cause. I must therefore conclude that the evil hand of Satan is upon them."

These words were greeted by a chorus of howls, shrieks, and barks.

Raising his voice above the din, Dr. Griggs went on: "But I am only a humble country doctor. For the love of truth call in some colleagues more learned than myself."

Thereupon he picked up his books and went off.

Suddenly there was silence in the room, as if Abigail and Betsey realized the formidableness of what had just been said. Then Betsey burst into pitiful sobs that seemed to combine fear, remorse, and infinite tiredness.

Samuel Parris came out onto the landing and with a shove sent me hard up against the wall. Then he walked up to me and gripped me by the shoulders. I hadn't realized how strong he was, with his hands like the claws of a bird of prey, and I had never been so close to the odor of his unwashed body.

"Tituba," he thundered, "if it is proved that you have bewitched my children, I'm telling you again, I shall have you hanged!"

I had the strength to protest. "Why is it you pick on me as soon as it's talk of spells? What about your neighbors? Mary Sibley seems to know quite a bit about them! Ask her!"

For I had begun to behave like an animal up against a wall, biting and scratching whoever she can.

Samuel Parris's face turned rigid and his mouth shrunk to a

thin, red line. He let go of me. "Mary Sibley?"

But it was written that he was not to seek an explanation from her, at least for the time being, for a pack of vixens came into the room downstairs, shouting that evil was on the loose and had afflicted other girls in the village. One after the other, Anne Putnam, Mercy Lewis, and Mary Walcott had fallen under what they had decided to call the devil's hand.

From the north to the south of Salem, over the wooden prisons of its houses, over the animal pens, its fields of juniper and daisies, there rose a muffled tumult of voices. Voices of the "possessed." Voices of terrified parents. Voices of servants or friends trying to bring relief. Samuel Parris seemed exhausted. "Tomorrow, I shall go to Boston to seek advice from the authorities."

What did I have to lose?

Picking up my skirt over the wooden clogs that made my feet bleed, I ran to the house of Thomas and Anne Putnam. Thomas Putnam was no doubt one of the richest men in Salem. This giant, awesome in his three-foot-wide hat and heavy cloth cape, made a strange contrast with his wife, who everyone agreed was mad. On more than one occasion, their daughter, little Anne Putnam, had spoken to me of her mother's wish to talk with me about her visions.

"What visions?"

"She sees people roasting in hell."

You can imagine that after such a conversation I preferred to avoid Anne Putnam altogether.

There were so many people at the Putnam's that nobody paid any attention to me and I could watch little Anne's capers unnoticed. At one moment she stood up straight, pointed her finger to the wall, and said in a theatrical tone of voice: "There he is! I can see him with his nose like an eagle's beak, his eyes like balls of fire, and his body covered with long hair. There he is! Look at him!"

You would have expected the crowd of adults not to take her seriously and to reassure the frightened child. Instead, the crowd ran in all directions, falling on their knees and reciting psalms and prayers. The only one to place her hands on her

Black Witch of Salem

hips and throw back her head to whinny in laughter was Sarah Good. She even went so far as to add: "Why not dance with him? If any of his creatures are in this room, you must be one of them!"

Then taking her little Dorcas by the hand, she stomped out. I should have done the same. On her departure, following these words of mockery, people started looking at their neighbors and I was discovered in a corner where I had taken refuge.

It was Goodwife Pope who threw the first stone. "A nice recruit Samuel Parris brought us back here! Instead of lining his pockets with gold he had to make do with this witch hazel."

Like so many other women in Salem, Goodwife Pope did not have a husband and she spent most of her time hawking a basket full of gossip from house to house. She always knew why such and such a baby had died and why such and such a wife's womb remained an empty gourd—generally, everyone kept well away from her. This time, however, everyone was behind her. Goodwife Hutchinson carried on where she had left off and picked up the second stone.

"As soon as he appeared in the village with these deathly faces in his baggage I knew he had opened misfortune's door. And now evil is upon us!"

What could I have said to defend myself?

To my surprise Goodwife Elizabeth Proctor, who was watching in the greatest affliction, dared to raise her voice: "Be careful not to condemn before the hour of judgment. We do not know whether it is witchcraft . . ."

Ten voices rose up over hers.

"Oh, yes we do! Oh, yes we do! Dr. Griggs said so!"

Goodwife Proctor bravely shrugged her shoulders. "Well, it won't be the first time we've seen a doctor make mistakes. Wasn't it this same Griggs who laid Nathaniel Bayley's wife in her grave while treating her throat when it was her blood that was poisoned?"

"Don't go to so much trouble for me, Goodwife Proctor," I said. "The spit of a toad never changed the scent of a rose." I know I could have chosen a better comparison and my enemies were quick to see it.

"Who's the rose?" they laughed outright. "You? You, Tituba? You've got your colors mixed up!"

⁂   ⁂   ⁂

Even if Mama Yaya and Abena, my mother, no longer spoke to me, I sensed they were there from time to time. Often in the morning a frail shadow would cling to the curtains in my room and then curl up at the bottom of my bed, communicating a mysterious warmth in an intangible way. I recognized Abena from the scent of honeysuckle that pervaded my wretched cubbyhole. Mama Yaya's perfume was stronger, almost spicy, but subtler. Mama Yaya did not convey any warmth but quickened my mind, convincing me that in the end nothing would be able to destroy me. In short, Mama Yaya brought me hope and Abena, my mother, tenderness. But understandably, faced with the serious dangers that were threatening me, I needed closer communication. With words. Sometimes nothing can replace words. Often deceitful, often treacherous, they nevertheless have an invariably soothing effect.

In a small enclosure behind our house I raised chickens in a coop that John Indian had built. I had often sacrificed them to my beloved spirits. For the time being, however, I needed other messengers. Two houses farther along, old Goody Hutchinson boasted a fine flock of sheep and one in particular that had an immaculate coat and a star marked on its forehead. At dawn, when a rooster crowed to the villagers of Salem that it was high time to honor their God by labor, a shepherd hired by Goody Hutchinson would set off, followed by two or three dogs, for the common grazing ground situated at the edge of the village. Goody Hutchinson had even had a few quarrels, since she refused to pay her grazing tithes. That was Salem! A community that stole, cheated, and burgled while wrapping itself in the cloak of God's name. And however much the burglars were branded with a **B**, were whipped or had their ears cut off or their tongues cut out, the crimes continued to increase!

In short, I had no scruples about robbing a thief.

I undid the rope of the pen and slipped in among the sleepy animals, which soon began to fret. I grabbed the one particular sheep. He began to shy away and arch his back, but I was the stronger and he had to follow me.

I dragged him to the edge of the forest.

For a short moment we stood looking at each other, he the victim, I the executioner but trembling and begging him to forgive me and to convey my prayers with the blood of the sacrifice. Then I slit his throat in one quick movement. He fell to his knees and the ground at my feet became moist. I anointed my forehead with the fresh blood. Then I gutted the animal, oblivious to the stench of entrails and excrement. I divided its flesh into four equal parts, which I presented to the four cardinal points, and then I left the flesh as an offering to my spirits.

After that I remained prostrate while prayers and incantations buzzed in my head. Would they finally speak to me, my life-giving forces? I needed them. I no longer had my island. I only had my man. I had had to kill my child. I needed them, they who had brought me into this world. I couldn't say how much time went by before there was a noise in the thickets. Mama Yaya and Abena, my mother, appeared in front of me. Were they at last about to break the wall of silence I kept running into? My heart was thumping.

Finally, it was Mama Yaya who spoke. "There's no need to be frightened, Tituba. Misfortune, as you know, is our constant companion. We are born with it, we lie with it, and we squabble with it for the same withered breast. It eats the codfish from our calabash. But we're tough, us niggers! And those who want to wipe us off the face of the earth will get their money's worth. Out of them all, you'll be the only one to survive."

"Will I return to Barbados?" I begged.

Mama Yaya shrugged her shoulders and merely said: "Is that really a question?"

Then with a slight wave of the hand she disappeared. Abena, my mother, stayed longer, uttering her usual quota of sighs. Then she too disappeared, without having brought any further clarification to the question.

I got up, somewhat reassured. The smell of blood and fresh

meat had started to attract some flies in spite of the cold. I went back to the village, where the roosters had already begun to crow. I hadn't realized I had spent so much time at my prayers. Sarah Hutchinson had just been roused from her bed by the shepherd, who had noticed the mainstay of the flock was missing and, hurriedly pushing her hair under her hood, she screamed out her rage.

"One day the vengeance of God will come down on the inhabitants of Salem as it did on Sodom, and as in Sodom there will not be ten just men to save the town from the supreme punishment. Thieves, den of thieves!"

Hypocritically, I even stopped to sympathize, and lowering her voice she drew me into a corner of the garden. "Help me, Tituba, to find the person who has done me wrong and punish him. Let his firstborn, if there is one, perish from something like smallpox. If there isn't a child yet, may his wife never bear one! I know you can do it! Everyone says you are the most awesome of witches!"

I looked her straight in the eyes with that fleeting arrogance infused in me by Mama Yaya and Abena, my mother, and said: "The most awesome are those that go unmentioned. You have lived long enough, Goody Hutchinson, to know you should not listen to hearsay."

She laughed wickedly. "You're very philosophical, my girl! You won't philosophize so much when you're swinging at the end of a rope!"

I couldn't help shivering and went home.

You may be surprised that I shiver at the idea of death. But that's the ambiguity of people like us. Our body is mortal and we are therefore prey to every torment of the common mortal. Like them, we fear suffering. Like them, we are frightened of the terrible antechamber that ends our life on earth. However certain we are that the doors will open before us onto another form of life, this time eternal, we are nevertheless racked with anguish.

In order to bring peace back into my heart and mind I had to repeat Mama Yaya's words: "Out of them all, you'll be the only one to survive."

II

I

Like three great birds of prey the three ministers sat themselves
down in the dining room. One had come from the parish of
Beverley, the other two from the town of Salem. They stretched
out their boney legs toward the fire that was crackling in
the hearth, then toasted the palms of their hands. Finally the
youngest, Samuel Allen, looked up at Samuel Parris and asked:
"Where are the children?"
"They're waiting upstairs," he replied.
"Are they all here?"
Samuel Parris nodded. "I asked their parents to bring them
here early. The parents are in the meeting house, praying."
The three ministers stood up. "Let us do the same, for the
task incumbent upon us requires the help of God."
Samuel Parris opened his book and started declaiming in his
grandiloquent way: "Thus saith the Lord, The heaven is my
throne, and the earth is my footstool: Where is the house that
ye build unto me? And where is my place of rest? For all those
things hath mine hand made . . ." He went on reading for a good
many minutes, then closed his book and said: "Isaiah 66."
It was Edward Payson from Beverley who ordered: "Bring
them down!"
As Samuel Parris was hurriedly leaving the room, he turned
to me and said in an unusually good-natured voice: "If you are
innocent you have nothing to fear."
I wanted my answer to sound firm, but it came out hoarse
and shaky: "I am innocent."
The children had begun filing into the room. Samuel Parris
had not told the truth when he claimed that they were all there,
for only Betsey, Abigail, and Anne Putnam were present. Then
I realized he had selected the youngest of the afflicted, as they

I, Tituba

were called, the ones most appealing to the heart of a father or a husband, whose only wish would be to relieve the girls' suffering and put an end to their torment.

I thought that except for Betsey, who was so frail and terrified, Abigail and Anne had never looked in better shape, especially Abigail who had that cunning air of a cat about to pounce on a defenseless bird.

I knew, of course, that I was the victim, but the impression I had was indescribable. There was rage. There was a desire to kill. There was pain, especially pain. I was the poor idiot who had sheltered these vipers in her bosom, offering up my breast to their triangular-shaped jaws and their forked tongues. I had been cheated. I had been ransomed like a galleon laden with pearls from Venice. A Spanish pirate was piercing my body with his sword.

Edward Payson, who was the oldest of the four men, to judge by his graying hair and withered skin, asked the first question. "Tell us, who, who is tormenting you, so that we can try to relieve you?"

With a pause calculated to give more weight to their words they cried: "It's Tituba!"

Amidst the turmoil of my feelings I heard them give other names linked to mine for no understandable reason. "There's Sarah Good! And Sarah Osborne!"

Sarah Good, Sarah Osborne, and I had hardly exchanged a word since we had been living in Salem. The most I had done was to give little Dorcas Good a piece of apple or pumpkin pie when she went by my window with that look of an undernourished child.

*   *   *

Like four great birds of prey the men surged into my room. They had slipped on black hoods, with holes for their eyes, and the steam from their mouths came through the cloth. Quickly they encircled the bed. Two seized my arms, while a third tied my legs so tight that I cried out in pain. Then one of them spoke and I recognized the voice of Samuel Parris.

"May something good at least come out of the hell you have unleashed. It would be easy for us to do away with you. Nobody in this village would lift a finger and the magistrates in Boston have better things to do. Besides, this is what we'll do if you don't obey us. For you're not worth the rope to hang you with!"

"What do you want me to do?" I stammered.

One of them sat down on the edge of the bed and, leaning over close enough to touch me, he snarled: "When you appear in front of the court, confess that this is your doing!"

"Never! Never!" I screamed.

The blow struck me across the mouth and drew blood. "Confess that this is your doing, but that you did not act alone and denounce your accomplices! Good and Osborne and the others!"

"I have no accomplice, since I have done nothing."

One of the men sat squarely astride me and began to hammer my face with his fists, which were as hard as stones. Another lifted up my skirt and thrust a sharpened stick into the most sensitive part of my body, taunting me: "Go on, take it, it's John Indian's prick."

When I was nothing more than a heap of suffering, they stopped, and one of the four spoke up again: "You are not the only creature of the Antichrist in Salem. There are others, do you hear, whose names you will give to the magistrate."

I finally began to realize what their intentions were. "Haven't your children already given the names of my so-called accomplices?" I said in a dying voice. "What more can I say?"

They laughed.

"Children talk in childish ways. We shall soon teach them not to forget the important points. And you'll be the first lesson."

I shook my head. "Never! Never!"

So they pounced on me again and it seemed as if the sharpened stick went right up to my throat. I held myself together, however, and groaned: "Never! Never!"

They consulted each other, then the door creaked and a voice called softly to me: "Tituba."

It was John Indian. The four birds of prey pushed him forward.

"You tell her, you seem less stubborn!"

They withdrew, leaving only our pain and the smell of my humiliation in the room.

John Indian hugged me and how sweet it was to be back in his arms. He tried to dab the blood from my wounds with his handkerchief. He pulled my skirt down over my violated thighs and I felt his tears on my skin.

"Wife, my tortured wife! Once again you're making a mistake about what matters most. The important thing is to stay alive. If they ask you to denounce the others, denounce them! Give the names of half of Salem, if that's what they want! This world is not ours and if they want to set it on fire, our job is to stay away from the flames. Denounce anybody they tell you to!"

I pushed him away. "John Indian, they want me to confess my faults. But I am not guilty."

He shrugged his shoulders and took me in his arms again, cradling me like an unruly baby. "Guilty? Oh, yes, you are and you always will be in their eyes. The important thing is to keep yourself alive for yourself, for me . . . and for our unborn children!"

"John Indian, don't talk about our children, for I shall never bring children into this dark and gloomy world."

He ignored this remark and went on. "Denounce them, my ravished wife! And by pretending to obey them, avenge yourself and me as well. Like the Lord, deliver up for plunder their mountains, their fields, their wealth, and their treasures."

* * *

Like three great birds of prey the constables from the village arrested Sarah Good, Sarah Osborne, and me. Oh, they had nothing to boast about, for none of us put up any resistance.

While placing her wrists in the chains, Sarah Good merely asked: "Who's going to look after Dorcas?"

The Proctors, who were present at the scene, came forward, their hearts filled with pity. "Go in peace. We shall take her in with our children."

On hearing this, the crowd let out a murmur as if everyone

was of the opinion that the child of a witch was no company for healthy children. Didn't the Proctors have some dubious contact with Sarah Good? And some people recalled that according to their servant, Mary Warren, Elizabeth Proctor stuck pins in wax dolls that she locked away in a cupboard. The constables then placed such heavy chains on our ankles and wrists that we could hardly move and we were dragged off to the prison in Ipswich.

It was February, the coldest month of a year without grace. A crowd had gathered along the main street in Salem to watch us leave. The constables rode ahead while we slid around in the snow and mud on the road. In the midst of all this desolation, surprisingly enough, we could hear the birds singing and hopping from branch to branch in the ice-colored air.

I recalled John Indian's words and now understood their profound wisdom. How naive I had been to think that proclaiming one's innocence would suffice to prove it. How naive I had been not to know that to do good to the evil and weak is the same as doing evil! Yes, I was going to take my revenge. I was going to denounce them and from the pinnacle of these powers they accorded me I was going to unleash the storm, whip up the sea with waves as high as walls, and toss the beams of the houses and barns into the air like straws.

Whose names did they want me to give?

Because I wasn't just going to give the names of the poor wretches who were being dragged along with me in the mud. I was going to strike hard. And at the top. And now that I was totally destitute, the feeling of power went to my head! Yes, my John Indian was right. This revenge, of which I had often dreamed, would now be mine and through the very doing of my enemies!

Ipswich was about ten miles from Salem and we arrived just before dusk fell. The jail was full of criminals, murderers, and thieves of all kinds that the land of Massachusetts bred in numbers as great as the number of fish in the sea.

A constable with a face as red as an apple from drinking too many mugs of rum registered our names in his book, then looked at a board behind him. "Only one cell left, witches! You can hold your meetings with no harm done. Satan must be with you!"

His colleagues gave him a look of reproach, as if this were no joking matter. But drink had put him in a higher sphere and he paid them no attention.

They piled us in one against the other and I had to put up with Sarah Good's stinking pipe as well as with the lugubrious prayers of Sarah Osborne, who was terrified. About midnight we were awakened by a clamor. "She's got me, she's got me! Let go of me, creature of Satan!"

It was Sarah Osborne whose eyes were bulging out of her head. Who was she pointing her finger at? Well, me of course! I turned to Sarah Good as a witness to our companion's audacity and hypocrisy. Was this how she was going to make her defense at my expense? And now she in turn started to scream, staring at me with her little pig eyes.

"She's got me, she's got me! Let go of me, creature of Satan!"

The constable with the red cheeks, who was by now completely drunk, put an end to this hellish pandemonium by kicking me violently out of the cell. Then he chained me to a hook in the passageway.

The bitter wind of night blew through all the keyholes.

2

We stayed a week in prison, awaiting the final preparations for our hearing before the court of Salem. And here again, despite my recent misfortunes and John Indian's recommendations, I fell into the trap of making friends. While I was shivering and losing my blood in the passageway where I had been chained, a woman passed her hands through the bars of her cell and stopped one of the constables.

"There's room here for two. Let that poor creature come in."

The woman who had spoken was young, beautiful, and not more than twenty-three. She had thrown back her hood unashamedly and revealed a mass of thick hair, as black as a crow's wing, itself the color of sin for some people and worthy of punishment. Likewise, her eyes were black, not the gray color of dirty water, not the green color of wickedness, but black like the benevolent shadow of night. She fetched some water in a jar and, bending down, endeavored to wash the welts on my face. While she did so, she thought to herself out loud: "What a magnificent color she's got for her skin and what a wonderful way she has of covering up her feelings! Fear, torment, rage, disgust! I've never managed to hide my feelings and my moods have always betrayed me!"

I stopped the movement of her hand. "Mistress . . ."

"Don't call me mistress."

"What shall I call you then?"

"By my name: Hester. And what's yours?"

"Tituba."

"Tituba?" She repeated it with delight. "Who gave it to you?"

I, Tituba

"My father gave it to me when I was born."

"Your father?" Her lip curled up in irritation. "You accepted the name a man gave you?"

I was so taken aback it took me a few moments to reply. "Isn't it the same for every woman? First her father's name, then her husband's?"

"I was hoping," she said musingly, "that at least some societies were an exception to this law. Yours, for example!"

It was my turn to muse. "Perhaps in Africa where we come from it was like that. But we know nothing about Africa any more and it no longer has any meaning for us."

As she walked up and down in the narrow cell, I saw that she was pregnant. I was still in a stupor when she came back up to me and asked softly: "Why were they calling you a witch?"

Once again, swept up in a wave of sympathy for this unknown woman, I made up my mind to explain. "Why, in your society . . ."

She interrupted me violently. "It's not my society. Aren't I an outcast like yourself? Locked up between these walls?"

I corrected myself. "Why in *this* society does one give the function of witch an evil connotation? The witch, if we must use this word, rights wrongs, helps, consoles, heals . . ."

She interrupted me with a burst of laughter. "Then you haven't read Cotton Mather!"

She puffed herself up and solemnly declared: "Witches do strange and evil things. They cannot perform true miracles; these can only be accomplished by the visible saints and emissaries of the Lord."

I laughed in turn and asked: "Who is this Cotton Mather?"

She did not answer; instead she took my face between her hands. "You cannot have done evil, Tituba! I am sure of that, you're too lovely! Even if they all accused you, I would defend your innocence!"

I was so moved I was bold enough to caress her face and whispered: "You too, Hester, are lovely! What are they accusing you of?"

"Adultery!" she said quickly.

I looked at her in alarm, for I knew the seriousness of such an offense in the eyes of the Puritans.

She went on: "And while I am rotting here the man who put this child in my womb is free to come and go as he pleases."

"Why don't you denounce him?" I whispered.

She spun round. "Ah, you haven't experienced the pleasure of revenge!"

"Revenge? I must confess I don't understand."

"Believe me, of the two of us," she said fervently, "I'm not the one to be most pitied. At least that's what you would expect from a man of God, if he has a conscience."

I was more and more puzzled. She must have realized it, because she came and sat down next to me on the filthy bedding.

"Perhaps I should start at the beginning if I want you to understand something of my story." She breathed in deeply and I settled down to listen. "In the bowels of the *Mayflower*, the first ship to have landed on this coast, were my two ancestors, my father's father and my mother's father, two fervent Separatists who had come to build the kingdom of the true God. You know how dangerous such projects are. No need to describe the fanaticism in which their descendants were brought up. It produced a flock of ministers who read Cicero, Cato, Ovid, and Virgil in the original . . ."

"I've never heard of these people," I interrupted.

She raised her eyes upward. "Thank goodness for that! I had the misfortune to belong to a family that believed in sexual equality and at the age when you normally play with dolls my father had me recite the classics! Now, where was I? Ah yes, at sixteen I was married to a minister, a friend of the family who had laid to rest three wives and five children. His breath was so awful that I was lucky enough to faint as soon as he leaned over me. He revolted me and yet he gave me four children that the good Lord called to him, thank God, for I would have found it impossible to love the offspring of a man I hated. I'll let you in on a secret, Tituba. The number of potions, concoctions, purges, and laxatives I took during my pregnancies helped me to arrive at this fortunate conclusion."

"I, too, killed my child," I whispered to myself.

"Luckily, a little over a year ago, he left for Geneva to confer with other Calvinists on the problem of the visible saints and it was then that . . ."

She stopped and I understood that despite her bluster she still loved her tormentor.

She went on: "There is something indecent about beauty in a man. Tituba, men shouldn't be beautiful! Two generations of visible saints stigmatizing carnal pleasure resulted in this man and the irresistible delights of the flesh. We started meeting under the pretext of discussing German pietism. Then we ended up in his bed making love and here I am!"

She folded her hands over her belly, and I asked: "What's going to happen now?"

She shrugged her shoulders. "I don't know. I think they're waiting for my husband to get back before deciding on my fate."

"What punishment are you likely to get?" I insisted.

She got up. "They no longer stone adulterous women. I believe they wear a scarlet letter on their breast."

It was my turn to shrug my shoulders. "Is that all they do?" But I was ashamed of my frivolousness when I saw the expression on her face. This woman, who was as good as she was beautiful, was suffering martyrdom. She was yet another case of a victim being branded guilty. Are women condemned to such a fate in this world? I looked for some way to give her hope again and whispered: "Aren't you pregnant? You must live for your child."

She shook her head firmly. "She must simply die with me. I have already prepared her for that when we talk to each other at night. You know, she's listening to us right now. She's just knocked on the door of my womb to get my attention. You know what she wants? She wants you to tell her a story. A story about your country. Make her happy, Tituba."

Resting my head against this soft curve of flesh, this hummock of life, so that the little one inside could be near my lips, I started to tell a tale and the familiar words of that ever-present, beloved ritual lit up the sadness of our confinement.

Crick, crack! Is the court asleep? No, the court isn't asleep! If the court isn't asleep, then listen, listen to this story, my story. Long long time ago, when the devil was still in short pants, showing his knobbly knees covered with scars, there lived in the village of Wagabaha, at the top of a pointed hill, a young girl who had neither father nor mother. A hurricane had blown away her parents' house and, miracle of miracles, had left the baby floating in her cradle like Moses on the waters. She was sad and lonely.

One day while she was taking her seat in the pew at church, she saw a tall black man standing near the pulpit dressed in white drill and wearing a straw hat with a black ribbon. Oh God, why can't women do without men? Why oh why?

"O dearly departed father, O dearly departed mother, I must have this man, otherwise I'll die."

"Do you know if he's good, if he's bad, if he's even human and has blood in his veins? Perhaps it's some evil-smelling, viscous humor that's flowing to his heart."

"O dearly departed father, O dearly departed mother, I must have him, otherwise I'll die."

"Well, if you want him, then you shall have him!"

And the young girl left her solitude and her cabin for the unknown man in white drill and slowly her life became hell on earth. Can't we ever keep our daughters away from men?"

Here Hester interrupted me, aware of the tremor in my voice. "What's this story you're telling me, Tituba? It's yours isn't it? Do tell me!"

But something kept me from telling her.

Hester taught me to prepare my testimony. Trust a minister's daughter to know a thing or two about Satan! Hadn't she eaten at his table since childhood? Hadn't he sprawled on her eiderdown in her cheerless bedchamber, staring at her with his yellowish eyes? Hadn't he meowed in every black cat? Croaked in every frog? And even danced in every gray mouse?

"Make them scared, Tituba! Give them their money's worth!

I, Tituba

Describe him as a billy goat with an eagle's beak for a nose, a body covered in long black hair with a belt of scorpion heads around his waist. Let them tremble, let them quake and swoon. Let them dance to the sound of his flute in the distance. Tell them about the witches' meetings, where they all arrive on broomsticks, their jaws dripping with anticipation at the thought of a feast of fetus and newly born babies served with many a mug of fresh blood."

I burst out laughing. "Now look, Hester, all this is ridiculous."

"No it isn't, because they believe it. What does it matter to you? Describe it!"

"Do you, too, advise me to give names?"

She frowned. "Who gave you that advice?"

I did not answer and she said earnestly: "Give names, give names! If you do you'll become the same as they are with a heart full of filth! If some of them have wronged you in person, then take your revenge, if that's what you want. Otherwise give them an element of doubt and, believe me, they'll know how to fill in the blanks! At the right moment shout: 'Oh, I can't see any more! I've gone blind!' And you'll have pulled the trick off."

"Oh!" I said fiercely, "I'll take my revenge on Sarah Good and Sarah Osborne, who denounced me for no reason whatsoever."

"Oh, yes, do that!" she laughed. "They're too ugly to live anyway. Now let's start our lesson over again. What does Satan look like? Don't forget he has more than one disguise up his sleeve. That's why after all this time nobody's caught him yet. Sometimes he's a black man . . ."

There I interrupted her in a worried voice. "If I say that, won't they think of John Indian?"

She shrugged her shoulders irritably. Hester got irritated easily. "Don't talk to me about your wretched husband! He's no better than mine. Shouldn't he be here to share your sorrow? Life is too kind to men, whatever their color."

I avoided talking to Hester about John Indian because I knew only too well what she would say and I wouldn't be able to stand it. However, something deep inside me told me she was telling the truth. The color of John Indian's skin had not caused him half the trouble mine had caused me. Some of the ladies, however Puritan they might be, had not denied themselves the pleasure of flirting with him.

"John Indian, they say you sing so well, and not only psalms!"

"Me, mistress?"

"Oh, yes, when you're digging at Deacon Ingersoll's they say you sing and dance at the same time."

And, perhaps unjustly, a bitterness grew inside me. When we were not rehearsing my testimony, Hester and I talked about ourselves. Oh how I loved to hear her talk! "I'd like to write a book, but alas, women don't write books! Only men bore us with their prose. I make an exception for certain poets. Have you read Milton, Tituba? Oh I forgot you don't know how to read. *Paradise Lost*, Tituba, a marvel of its kind. . . . Yes, I'd like to write a book where I'd describe a model society governed and run by women! We would give our names to our children, we would raise them alone . . ."

I interrupted her, poking fun: "We couldn't make them alone, even so!"

"Alas, no," she said sadly. "Those abominable brutes would have to share in a fleeting moment."

"Not too short a moment," I teased. "I like to take my time."

She ended up laughing and drew me close to her.

"You're too fond of love, Tituba! I'll never make a feminist out of you!"

"A feminist? What's that?"

She hugged me in her arms and showered me with kisses. "Be quiet! I'll explain later."

Later? Would there be a later? The day was coming when we would be taken to Salem to be judged and then what would happen to us?

However much Hester repeated that there was a law in Massachusetts that spared the life of a witch if she confessed, I was frightened.

Sometimes my fear was like a baby in its mother's womb.

I, Tituba

It turns from left to right, then kicks around. Sometimes my fear was like a wicked bird tearing out my liver with its beak. Sometimes it was like a boa constrictor suffocating me with its coils. I had heard that the meeting house in Salem had been enlarged to make room for the villagers as well as the people from the surrounding area who wanted to take part in the festivities. I had heard that they had built a platform on which Sarah Good, Sarah Osborne, and I would stand, so that everyone could feast their eyes on the spectacle. I had heard that arbitrators had been appointed, members of the Massachusetts General Court, known for their integrity and firm beliefs: John Hathorne and Jonathan Corwin.

What could I possibly hope for? Even if they left me my life, what would it be worth to me? Could John Indian and I free ourselves from our bondage and set sail on a ship bound for Barbados?

I am back on the island I thought I had lost! No less rust-colored, her soil! No less green, her hills! No less mauve, her sugarcane, sticky with juice. No less satiny the emerald belt around her waist! But the men and women are suffering. They are in torment. A slave has just been hung from the top of a flame tree. The blossom and the blood have merged into one. I have forgotten that our bondage is not over. They are lopping off our ears, legs, and arms. They are sending us up in the air like fireworks. Look at the confetti made with our blood!

When I was in this mood, Hester could not do anything for me. No matter how much she tried to reassure me, I did not listen. So she would slip between my lips a little rum that one of the constables had given her, and gradually I would doze off. Mama Yaya and Abena, my mother, would then appear one after the other and repeat tenderly: "Why are you shaking? Haven't we told you that you will be the only one to survive?"

Perhaps. But life scared me just as much as death, especially as I was so far from my people.

Despite my friendship with Hester, the prison left an indelible impression on me. This somber flower of the civilized world poisoned me with its perfume and I could never again breathe the same way. Encrusted in my nostrils was the smell of so many crimes: matricides, parricides, rapes, thefts, manslaughter, murders, and above all the smell of so much suffering.

On 29 February we started back on the road to Salem. Throughout the journey Sarah Good pelted me with abuse and curses. You would think it was my presence alone that had caused so much evil in Salem.

"Why did you leave your hell, Negress?"

I hardened my heart. I would get my revenge very soon on that woman!

3

Deposition of Tituba Indian[*]
"Tituba, what evil spirit have you familiarity with?"
"None."
"Why do you hurt these children?"
"I do not hurt them."
"Who is it then?"
"The devil for aught I know."
"Did you never see the devil?"
"The devil came to me and bid me serve him."
"Who have you seen?"
"Four women sometimes hurt the children."
"Who were they?"
"Sarah Osborne and Sarah Good, and I do not know who the others were. Sarah Good and Osborne would have me hurt the children, but I would not. There was also a tall man of Boston."
"When did you see them?"
"Last night at Boston."
"What did they say to you?"
"They said 'Hurt the children.' "
"And did you hurt them?"
"No, there were four women and one man, they hurt the children, and then they lay all upon me; and they tell me, if I will not hurt the children, they will hurt me."
"But did you not hurt them?"

---

[*] These extracts are taken from the deposition of Tituba Indian. The original documents of the trial are kept in the Essex County Archives. A copy can be found at the Essex County Courthouse, Salem, Massachusetts.

Black Witch of Salem

"Yes, but I will hurt them no more."

"Are you not sorry that you did hurt them?"

"Yes."

"And why then do you hurt them?"

"They said 'Hurt the children or we will do worse to you.' "

"What have you seen?"

"A man came to me and said 'Serve me.' "

"What service?"

"Hurt the children; and last night there was an appearance that said 'Kill the children'; and if I would not go on hurting the children, they would do worse to me."

"What is this appearance you see?"

"Sometimes it is like a hog, and sometimes like a great dog."

"What did it say to you?"

"The black dog said, 'Serve me,' but I said, 'I am afraid.' He said if I did not, he would do worse to me."

"What did you say to it?"

" 'I will serve you no longer.' Then he said he would hurt me; and then he looked like a man and threatened to hurt me. This man had a yellow bird that kept with him. And he told me he had more pretty things that he would give me if I would serve him."

"What were those pretty things?"

"He did not show them."

"What else have you seen?"

"Two rats; a red rat and a black rat."

"What did they say to you?"

"They said 'Serve me.' "

"When did you see them?"

"Last night; and they said 'Serve me,' but I said I would not."

"What service?"

"Hurt the children."

"Did you not pinch Elizabeth Hubbard this morning?"

"The man brought her to me and made me pinch her."

"Why did you go to Thomas Putnam's last night and hurt his child?"

"They pulled and hauled me and made me go."

"And what would they have you do?"

I, Tituba

"Kill her with a knife."

"How did you go?"

"We rode upon sticks and were there presently."

"Do you go through the trees or over them?"

"We see nothing but are there presently."

* * *

It went on for hours. I confess I wasn't a good actress. The sight of all these white faces lapping at my feet looked to me like a sea in which I was about to drown. Oh, Hester would have made a much better job of it than I! She would have used that tribunal to shout her hatred of society and to curse her accusers in return. I was truly quite scared out of my wits. The heroic answers I had dreamed up at home or in my cell vanished into thin air.

* * *

"Did you not see Sarah Good upon Elizabeth Hubbard last Saturday?"

"I did see her set a wolf upon her to afflict her."

"What clothes doth the man go in?"

"He goes in black clothes; a tall man, with white hair, I think."

"How doth the woman go?"

"In a white hood, and a black hood with a topknot."

"Do you see who it is that torments these children now?"

I spit out with delight and venom: "Yes, it is Goody Good; she hurts them in her own shape."

"Who is it that hurts them now?"

"I am blind now, I cannot see," I stuttered, remembering Hester's recommendations.

I didn't have the heart to obey Samuel Parris and give the names of innocent women.

* * *

After my examination, Samuel Parris came to see me. "Well spoken, Tituba. You understood what we expected of you."

I hate myself as much as I hate him.

4

I was not an eyewitness to the plague that afflicted Salem, because I was kept chained up in Deacon Ingersoll's barn after I had made my deposition.

*   *   *

Goodwife Parris very soon repented. She came to see me and wept. "Tituba, what have they done to you, to you the kindest of creatures?"

I tried to shrug my shoulders, but my chains held me too tightly. "Two weeks ago I heard a different story," I retorted.

She sobbed even louder. "I was misled, misled! I can see now what's behind it all! A plot by Parris and his followers to smear and ruin . . ."

I interrupted her, as this was of no interest to me. I heard myself say tenderly: "And Betsey?"

She looked up. "I have taken her away from this horrible carnival and sent her to Samuel Parris's half-brother, Stephen Sewall, who lives in the town of Salem. He's not like Samuel. He's a good man. I think that our little Betsey will recover her health with him. Before she left, she asked me to tell you that she loves you and she asks you to forgive her."

I didn't answer. Then Goodwife Parris told me what was going on in the village.

"I can only compare it to a sickness that first of all is thought to be benign because it affects the lesser parts of the body . . ."

Lesser parts? It's true I was only a black slave. It's true Sarah Good was a beggar. So great was her poverty that she had to abstain from coming to the meeting house for want of clothes. It's true that Sarah Osborne had a bad reputation because the Irish immigrant she had hired to help her on the farm quickly advanced from the widow's barn to her bed. But even so, it was shocking to hear us coldly described as "lesser parts."

Little suspecting the feelings she aroused in me, Goodwife Parris went on: ". . . then gradually attacks the limbs and vital organs. The arms and legs can no longer move. Then the heart is attacked and finally the brain. Martha Corey and Rebecca Nurse have been arrested!"

I opened my mouth in amazement. Goody Rebecca Nurse! It was incredible! She was the living image of God's faith!

Goodwife Parris continued: "Judge Hathorne himself was moved by her and the first jury gave a verdict of not guilty. But that wasn't enough it seems and she has been taken to town to appear before another court."

Her eyes filled with tears. "My poor Tituba, it was horrible! If you had seen Abigail and Anne Putnam, especially Anne Putnam, roll on the ground screaming that the poor old woman was tormenting her and begging her to have pity on them, your heart would have filled with doubt and horror. And she herself remained calm and serene while reciting the twenty-third psalm: 'The Lord is my shepherd; I shall not want. He maketh me to lie down in green pastures: he leadeth me beside the still waters. He restoreth my soul . . .' "

Hearing the ravages that evil was making in Salem, I was worried sick about John Indian.

There was so much talk about a "black man" who forced his victims to write in his book. Wouldn't a perverted mind be tempted to identify him with John Indian? And then he in turn would be persecuted. My worries, however, seemed unfounded. On the rare occasions when John Indian came into the barn where I lay groaning, he seemed in excellent health, well fed, his clothes washed and ironed. He was even wrapped in a thick, warm woolen cape. And I recalled Hester's words: "Life is too kind to men, whatever their color."

One day I plied him with questions.

"Don't you worry about me!" he said irritably.

But I insisted.

"I know how to get by," he blurted out.

"What do you mean?"

He spun round and stared at me. Oh, how changed he had become! He'd never been very brave or very intelligent or honest, but loving, yes! A cunning expression had changed his face, and his eyes now stretched into narrow slits with a crafty gleam in them.

"What do you mean?" I stammered again.

"I mean, my poor, suffering wife, that I am not like you. Do you think it's only Abigail, Anne Putnam, and the other bitches who know how to howl, have fits, faint, and pant: 'Ow! You're pinching me, you're hurting me! Let me go!' "

I looked at him a moment without fully understanding. Then it dawned on me.

"John Indian," I murmured. "You too are pretending to be tormented."

He nodded. "I had my hour of glory a few days ago," he boasted.

And he started to play in turn the magistrates and the girls sitting round in a semicircle:

"John Indian who is tormenting you?"

"Goodwife Proctor first of all and then Goody Cloyse."

"What do they do?"

"They bring me the devil's book."*

"John Indian, tell the truth, who is tormenting you?' For if anyone suspected me of evil-doing, it was Judge Danforth, the filthy racist!"

I was appalled. I was ashamed. But hadn't I been forced to lie to save my life? Was John Indian's lie any worse than my own?

* * *

And yet, however much I told myself this, from that day on, my feelings for John Indian started to change. For me it seemed he had made a pact with my tormentors. Who knows? If I had found myself on that infamous platform and had been treated as an object of contempt and terror by those despicable judges, amidst those feigned cries of affliction, wouldn't he have been

* Deposition of John Indian; Essex County Archives.

capable of shouting: "Oh, oh, Tituba is tormenting me! Yes, my wife is a witch!"

*   *   *

Did John Indian realize what I was feeling? Or was there another reason? Whatever the case, he stopped coming to visit me. I was taken back to Ipswich and I never saw him again.

When we reached the outskirts of Ipswich, the villagers of Topsfield, Beverley, Lynn, and Malden ran to the edge of the road to throw stones at me while I stumbled along, roped to Constable Herrick's saddle. The bare trees looked like wooden crosses and my calvary went on and on.

As I stumbled forward, I was racked by a violent feeling of pain and terror. It seemed that I was gradually being forgotten. I felt that I would only be mentioned in passing in these Salem witchcraft trials about which so much would be written later, trials that would arouse the curiosity and pity of generations to come as the greatest testimony of a superstitious and barbaric age. There would be mention here and there of "a slave originating from the West Indies and probably practicing 'hoodoo.'" There would be no mention of my age or my personality. I would be ignored. As early as the end of the seventeenth century, petitions would be circulated, judgments made, rehabilitating the victims, restoring their honor, and returning their property to their descendants. I would never be included! Tituba would be condemned forever! There would never, ever, be a careful, sensitive biography recreating my life and its suffering.

And I was outraged by this future injustice that seemed more cruel than even death itself.

We reached Ipswich in time to see a woman who had been sentenced for some crime or other swinging from the end of a rope and the crowd said it was only right and proper.

On entering the prison, my first thought was to ask to be with Hester in her cell. Oh, how right she had been about John Indian! He had been simply a pathetic individual without love or honor. Tears that only Hester would know how to dry welled up in my eyes.

But without looking up from his register, the constable, who was fond of rum, told me that being with Hester was out of the question.

"Why, why, Master?" I insisted in desperation.

He deigned to stop scribbling and stared at me. "It's out of the question because she's no longer here."

I remained speechless, imagining a thousand things in my head. Had she been pardoned? Had her husband come back from Geneva and freed her? Had she been taken to the alms-house to give birth? I had no idea how many months pregnant she was; perhaps her time was up?

"Master," I managed to stammer out, "have the goodness to tell me what has happened to her, for there is not a kinder soul on this earth!"

The constable snorted. "Kind? Well, however kind you may think she is, by now she's damned because she hanged herself in her cell."

"Hanged herself?"

"Yes, hanged herself!"

I screamed down the door of my mother's womb. My fist broke her bag of waters in rage and despair. I choked and suffocated in this black liquid. I wanted to drown myself.

Hanged herself? Hester, Hester, why didn't you wait for me?

Mother, will our torture never end? If this is how things are, I shall never emerge into the light of day. I shall remain crouched in your waters, deaf, dumb, and blind, clinging like kelp to your womb. I shall cling so tightly you'll never expel me and I shall return to dust without you, without ever having known the curse of day. Mother, help me!

Hanged herself? Hester, I would have gone with you.

After much deliberation by the authorities, I was taken to the almshouse in the town of Salem because no such institution existed in Ipswich. At first I could make no distinction between night and day. Both were blurred in the same circle of pain. They had left me in shackles, not because they feared I would take my life, which would have been a happy ending for all, but because I might attack my companions in misfortune in a fit of rage. A certain Doctor Zerobabel came to see me because he was studying mental illnesses and hoped to be appointed professor at Harvard College. He suggested trying one of his potions on me: "Take the milk of a woman suckling a male child. Also take a cat and cut off its ear or part of it. Let the blood flow into the milk. Get the patient to drink this mixture. Repeat three times a day."

Whether it was the effect of this medication I do not know, but I went from a state of great agitation to a state of torpor. This change was taken to be the first sign of healing. I opened my eyes, which I had stubbornly kept closed. I agreed to accept food. However, I couldn't pronounce a single word.

Since the cost of my upkeep at the almshouse was too high and could no longer be paid for by the town of Salem, to which I belonged, they sent me to prison. I did not recognize a single face among the crowd there. It was as if everything before Hester's death had been wiped from my memory.

One morning, I don't know why exactly, my speech and memory came back to me. I asked for news about what was going on around me. I learned that Sarah Osborne had died in prison, but I felt no pity for her.

At this point in my life I was haunted by the temptation to kill myself. It seemed that Hester had set me an example to follow. Alas! I didn't have the courage.

I never understood why, but they transferred me from Ipswich to the town of Salem. I had fairly pleasant memories of this town, which I had visited a long time before with Samuel Parris and his family. This port on a narrow peninsula squeezed between two lazy rivers rivaled Boston, and the wharfs bristled with ships. Yet there was (and this was intensified by my state of mind) a cloud of gloom and austerity that floated over the houses. We passed by the schoolhouse with a yard in front where melancholy schoolboys, waiting to be whipped by their masters, were tied to posts. In the middle of Court Street a massive building rose up whose stones had been brought at great expense from England and where man's justice was handed out. A crowd of men and women, dark and silent, stood under the building's arcades. The jail itself was a gloomy building with a thatched, log roof and an iron-plated door.

5

I often think of Hester's child and of my own. Those unborn
children. It was for their own good we denied them the light
of day and the salty taste of their skin under the sun. Children
we spared, but whom, strangely enough, I pity. Were they boys
or girls? What does it matter really? I shall sing my old lament
for both of them.

> The moonstone dropped into the water,
> Into the waters of the river,
> And my fingers couldn't reach it,
> Woe is me!
> The moonstone has fallen.
> Sitting on a rock on the riverbank
> I wept and I lamented.
> Oh, softly shining stone,
> Glimmering at the bottom of the water.
> The hunter passed that way
> With his bow and arrows.
> "Why are you crying, my lovely one?"
> "I'm crying because my moonstone
> Lies at the bottom of the water."
> "If it is but that, my lovely,
> I will help you."
> But the hunter dived and was drowned.

Hester, my heart is breaking.

One morning, as if in mockery, they put a child in my cell.
At first I did not recognize her, so blurred were my eyes with
suffering. Then my memory came back to me. Dorcas Good!
It was the little four-year-old Dorcas, whom I had always seen

I, Tituba

hiding in her mother's dirty skirts until a constable separated mother and child.

The band of little vixens had denounced her and men had shackled the arms, wrists, and ankles of this innocent child. I was too engrossed in my own misfortune to pay attention to that of others, but the sight of this little girl brought tears to my eyes.

She looked at me and said: "Do you know where my mother is?"

I had to confess I didn't. Had she already been hanged? The rumor in prison had it that she had given birth to another child, a boy, a son of the devil, who had returned to hell where he belonged. I knew nothing else.

From that moment on, it was for Dorcas as well, daughter of a woman who had accused me so unjustly, that I sang my old lament, "The moonstone dropped into the water."

6

The plague that afflicted Salem very quickly spread to other villages and towns and one by one Amesbury, Topsfield, Ipswich, and Andover entered into the dance. Like hounds excited by the smell of blood, the constables prowled the country footpaths, hunting those whom our band of little vixens, with their gift of ubiquity, continued to denounce. I learned through prison rumors that so many children had been arrested they had been housed in a hastily built thatched log building. At night the noise of their shouting kept the inhabitants awake. I was taken out of my cell to make room for the accused who were thought worthy of a roof over their heads and it was from the prison courtyard that I now saw the cartloads of condemned prisoners rumble by. Some of the prisoners stood straight upright as if they were defying their judges. Others, however, groaned in terror and begged like children for one more day, one more hour.

I saw Rebecca Nurse led off to Gallows Hill and I recalled the time she had whispered in her shaky voice: "Can't you help me, Tituba?" I regretted I hadn't, because now I could see that her enemies had triumphed. I learned through prison rumor that those very same Houltons had unleashed the hogs of their wrath against her. Rebecca Nurse was clinging to the bars of the cart and staring at the sky as if she were trying to find an explanation.

I saw Sarah Good go by. She had evidently been kept in another building and was still wearing her vulgar smirk. She looked at me tied up to a post like an animal and shouted: "I prefer my fate to yours, you know!"

It was after the executions of 22 September that I was put back into a prison cell. The bedding seemed to me as soft as a feather and that night I dreamed of Mama Yaya with a garland of magnolia flowers around her neck. She repeated her promise: "You'll be the only one to survive," but I refrained from asking her "So what?"

Time stretched endlessly above our heads.

It's strange how human beings refuse to admit that they are beaten.

Stories started going around in prison. It was whispered that the children of Rebecca Nurse had found a sweet-smelling white rose in place of her body when they had come at dusk to remove their mother from the unmarked grave of shame where the executioner had thrown her. It was whispered that Judge Noyes, who had convicted Sarah Good, had died mysteriously in a pool of blood. There was talk of a strange illness that was striking down the families of the accusers and a good many were being laid to rest under the earth. There was talk and there were stories; and the stories were embellished. And they rose up into a muffled murmur of words, soft but tenacious, like the waves of the sea.

Perhaps it was these words that kept men, women, and children alive, that helped them to turn the grindstone of life. There was one incident, however, that cast a pall over people's minds. Although we had almost gotten used to seeing the cart of condemned women rumble past, the news that Giles Corey had been literally pressed to death filled us with horror. I never did like Giles Corey and his wife, Goody Martha, very much, especially because she had the unpleasant habit of mumbling a prayer whenever she met me. I had not even been upset when I learned that Giles had testified against me. Hadn't John Indian already betrayed me by joining the side of the accusers? But when I heard that this old man, who went from accuser to being the accused, had been staked out on his back in a field and the deputies had piled stone upon stone on his chest, it made me wonder about the kind of people who were convicting us. Where was Satan? Wasn't he hiding in the folds of the judges' coats? Wasn't he speaking in the voices of these magistrates and men of religion?

It was said that all Giles asked for was "more stones" to finish with it and to end his suffering. Soon there was a song about him: "Corey, O Corey, For you the stones have no weight, For you the stones are as light as a feather."

The second event, which was even more horrible than the first, was the arrest of George Burroughs. I have already said that George Burroughs had been minister in Salem before Samuel Parris and like Samuel Parris he had had no end of trouble getting the terms of his contract respected. It was one of his wives whose soul had departed from the upstairs bedchamber in our house. But hearing that this man of God had been accused of being Satan's henchman plunged the prison into dismay.

This God, for whom they had left the meadows and woods of England, was turning his back on them.

We learned, however, in early October that the governor of the colony, Governor Phips, had written to London asking for advice on legal procedures concerning witchcraft. Shortly afterward we heard that the court of oyer and terminer would no longer convene and that another court would meet where members would be less suspected of collusion with the accusers' families.

I have to confess this had little effect on me. I was condemned to live!

7

I hope that the generations to come will live under a welfare state that will truly provide for the well-being of its citizens. In 1692, at the time of our story, this was not the case. Be it in prison or almshouse, the state did not provide for you and, guilty or not guilty, you had to pay for your upkeep and the cost of your chains.

The accused were generally well-off, owners of land and farms that could be mortgaged. They had no difficulty, therefore, in meeting the requirements of the colony. Since Samuel Parris had made it known very early on that he had no intention of paying my prison costs, the superintendent decided he would get his money back by making me work in the kitchens.

The foulest food is always considered too good for a prisoner. Cartloads of vegetables were trundled into the prison courtyard and their lingering smell left no doubt about their rotting state. The cabbages were turning black, the carrots green, the sweet potatoes were crawling with maggots, and the ears of corn bought from the Indians at half price were full of borers. Once a week, on the Sabbath, the prisoners were treated to an ox bone boiled in gallons of water and served with dried apples. My job was to prepare this dismal food and I found myself remembering my old recipes in spite of myself. Cooking has the advantage of keeping the mind free while the hands are busy doing their own creative work. I cut up all this rotting food. I seasoned it with a sprig of mint growing haphazardly between two stones. I added what I could from an ill-smelling bunch of onions. I excelled in making cakes that, although a bit heavy, were nonetheless tasty.

Black Witch of Salem

How easily reputations are made! Soon, to my amazement, I was reputed to be an excellent cook and I was hired out for weddings and banquets.

I became a familiar figure ambling through the streets of Salem, going in through the back doors of houses and hotels. When they heard the jangling of my chains, the women and children would come out on their doorsteps to look. But I seldom heard jibes or jeers. Above all I was an object of pity.

I used to walk as far as the sea, which was almost hidden by the hulls of the brigantines, schooners, and other kinds of ships.

It was the sea that healed me.

Her great, wet hand pressed against my forehead. Her salts filled my nostrils. Her bitter potion moistened my lips. Gradually I pieced myself together. Gradually I picked up hope again. In what? I don't know exactly. But a gentle little expectation rose inside me like a sunrise. I learned through prison rumor that John Indian was in the front line of the accusers, that he accompanied the girls, those scourges of God, shouted when they shouted, had seizures when they had them, and gave names louder and stronger than they did. I learned that on the bridge at Ipswich it was John Indian who had screamed "witch!" at a poor wretch in rags, well before Anne Putnam and Abigail had done so. They even said he had pointed to Satan in the harmless shape of a cloud above the heads of the condemned prisoners.

What could I possibly feel on hearing this?

In May 1693 Governor Phips decreed a general pardon, after approval from London, and the prison gates opened for the accused witches of Salem. Fathers were reunited with their children, husbands with their wives, and mothers with their daughters. I was reunited with nobody. This pardon changed nothing as far as I was concerned. My fate passed unnoticed.

Noyes, the superintendent, came to see me. "Do you know how much you owe the colony?"

I shrugged my shoulders. "How could I?"

"It's all written down!" And he turned the pages of a book. "There, you see! Seventeen months of prison at two shillings and sixpence a week. Who's going to pay me that?"

I said I had no idea and then asked: "What are you going to do?"

"Find someone who'll pay the prison costs and at the same time employ you in his service!" he grumbled.

"Who's prepared to buy a witch?" I laughed scornfully.

He smiled cynically. "A man who hasn't got very much money. You know how much slaves are selling for at the present time? Twenty-five pounds!"

Our conversation stopped there, but now I knew the fate awaiting me. Another master, another bondage.

I began to doubt seriously Mama Yaya's basic conviction that life is a gift. Life would only be a gift if each of us could choose the womb that carried us. But to be deposited inside a wretch, an egoist, or a self-centered bitch who makes us pay for the misfortunes of her own life, or to belong to the cohort of the exploited and humiliated, those whose name, language, and religion are imposed upon them, oh what a martyrdom!

If one day I am born again, let it be in the steely army of conquerors!

Every day after that conversation with Noyes, complete strangers would come to examine me. They would inspect my gums and my teeth. They would pinch my stomach and my breasts. They would lift up my rags to examine my legs. Then they would make a face.

"She's terribly skinny!"

"You say she's twenty-five? She looks fifty!"

"I don't like her color!"

One afternoon I found grace in the eyes of a man. But my God, what a man! He was small and hunchbacked, with a complexion the color of eggplant and large, ginger-colored sidewhiskers that merged into a pointed beard.

Noyes whispered contemptuously: "He's a Jew, a merchant. They say he's very rich. He could afford a whole cargo of slaves and here he is haggling over a jailbird!"

I ignored his offensive remarks. A merchant? Probably trading with the West Indies? With Barbados?

Suddenly I looked at the Jew with new eyes, as if his downright ugliness had become the most appealing of assets. Didn't he symbolize the prospects I had dreamed of?

My eyes expressed such hope and desire that he turned round and hobbled off, probably mistaking the meaning of their transformation. I then saw that his right leg was shorter than his left.

Night, night, lovelier than day! Maker of dreams! A great crossroads where the present takes the past by the hand, where the living and the dead merge.

In this cell where there remained only poor Sarah Daston, who was now too old and too poor and would probably end her days between these walls, Mary Watkins, who was waiting for a buyer, and myself, whom nobody wanted, I managed to call on Mama Yaya and Abena, my mother. May their combined powers make me fall into the hands of that merchant whose look told me that he, too, was from the land of the suffering and that in some undefinable way, we were, or we could be, on the same side.

Barbados!

During the periods of my sickness with its fever and stupor I had given very little thought to my native land. But once I had precariously pieced myself together, the memory of it came back to me.

Yet the news I had of the island was not good. An empire of suffering and humiliation had been staked out there. The wretched herd of slaves continued to turn the wheel of misfortune. Grind my forearm, mill, with the sugarcane so that my blood colors the sweet juice.

And that wasn't all!

Every day other islands round about were being opened up to the appetite of the white man and I learned that in the colonies of South America our hands were now weaving long cotton shrouds.

That night I had a dream.

My ship was entering the harbor, its sails swelling with all my impatience. I was on the wharf watching the tarred prow cut through the water. At the foot of one of the masts I could make out a shape that I was unable to name, but I knew it was bringing me joy and happiness. How long would it be before I enjoyed such a truce? That I couldn't guess. I knew that fate is like an old man. It toddles along. It stops to catch its breath. It sets off again. It stops once more. It reaches its destination in its own time. But I had the feeling that the darkest hours were behind me and I would soon be able to breathe again.

That night Hester lay down beside me, as she did sometimes. I laid my head on the quiet water lily of her cheek and held her tight. Surprisingly, a feeling of pleasure slowly flooded over me. Can you feel pleasure from hugging a body similar to your own? For me, pleasure had always been in the shape of another body whose hollows fitted my curves and whose swellings nestled in the tender flatlands of my flesh. Was Hester showing me another kind of bodily pleasure?

* * *

Three days later Noyes came and opened the door of my cell. Behind him, in his shadow, crept the Jew, more ginger-colored and crooked than ever. Noyes pushed me as far as the prison courtyard, where the blacksmith, a huge man in a leather apron, unceremoniously drew my legs apart with two blocks of wood. Then with one skillful blow of the mallet he smashed my chains to pieces. He did the same thing with my wrists while I screamed.

I screamed while my blood, which for so many weeks had circulated poorly, rushed back into my flesh, pricking my skin with a thousand darts.

I screamed, and this scream, the terrified cry of a newborn baby, heralded my return to this world. I had to learn how to walk again. Deprived of my shackles, I was unable to find my balance and I tottered like a woman drunk on cheap liquor. I had to learn how to speak again, how to communicate with my fellow creatures, and no longer be content with a word here and there. I had to learn how to look them in the eyes again. I had to learn how to do my hair again now that it had become a tangle of untidy snakes hissing around my head. I had to rub ointments on my dry, cracked skin, which had become like a badly tanned hide.

Few people have the misfortune to be born twice.

8

Benjamin Cohen d'Azevedo, the Jew who had just bought me, had lost his wife and his youngest children in an epidemic of whooping cough. He still had five girls and four boys who urgently needed the company of a woman. Since he did not intend to remarry, as all the other men in the colony did in such cases, he preferred to have a slave.

I was therefore confronted with nine children of varying sizes, some with hair as black as a magpie's tail, others as ginger-colored as their father, all of whom had the particularity of not speaking one word of English. Benjamin's family had come from Portugal, where religious persecution had forced them to flee to Holland. From there, one branch of the family had tried for Brazil, Recife to be exact, but had to flee once again when the town was recaptured by the Portuguese. They then split into two clans, one settling in Curaçao, the other trying its luck in the American colonies. And their ignorance of the English language and this constant babble in Hebrew and Portuguese showed how indifferent this family was to the misfortunes of others and to anything that did not concern the tribulations of Jews the world over. I wondered if Benjamin Cohen d'Azevedo had even heard about the Salem witch trials and whether he hadn't entered the prison by accident. In any case, if he had heard about those sad events, he would have put them down to the basic cruelty that seemed to characterize those he called Gentiles and would have forgiven me entirely. In a way I couldn't have fallen into better hands.

The only visitors who crept into Benjamin Cohen d'Azevedo's home were half a dozen other Jews who came to celebrate the Saturday ritual. I learned that they had been refused permission to build a synagogue. So they huddled together in one room of the large house facing a seven-branched candelabrum and murmuring mysterious words in a monotonous voice. On Friday nights no light could be lit and the troop of children ate, washed, and went to bed in total darkness.

Benjamin Cohen d'Azevedo was in constant touch by letter and trade with other Cohens, Levys, and Fraziers who lived in New York (which he insisted on calling New Amsterdam!) and Rhode Island. He earned a comfortable living from the tobacco trade and owned two ships in association with his fellow Jew and friend Judah Monis. Benjamin was a man of considerable wealth, but little vanity, tailoring his clothes himself from pieces of cloth from New York and living off unleavened bread and gruel. The day after I entered his service, he held out a flat vial and said in his squeaky voice: "It was my beloved Abigail who used to prepare this. It'll put you back on your feet."

Then he went off with his eyes lowered, as if he were ashamed of the goodness of his heart. That same day he brought me clothes of dark cloth and an unusual cut. "Here, these belonged to my beloved Abigail. I know that where she is now she would like you to wear them."

It was beloved Abigail who brought us together.

She started by weaving between us a tissue of little acts of kindness, little services, and little signs of recognition. Benjamin would slice an orange from the islands for Metahebel, his eldest daughter, and me. He would invite me to drink a glass of hot toddy with his friends or throw an extra blanket over me when it was too cold in my attic at night. I would iron his rough shirts carefully, brush and clean his cape that was green with wear, and spice his milk with honey. On the first anniversary of his wife's death he looked so desperate that I couldn't help saying softly: "You know that death is merely a passageway and the door always remains open?"

He looked at me in disbelief.

I grew bolder and whispered: "Do you want to speak to her?"

He rolled his eyes back.

"This evening," I ordered, "when the children are asleep,

join me in the orchard. Bring a sheep or, if there is none, a chicken from your friend the shohet."

I must confess that despite my apparent self-assurance, my heart was in my throat. It had been such a long time since I had practiced my art! In the promiscuous conditions of the prison, among my companions in ill fortune, and deprived of any natural element to help me, I had never been able to communicate with my invisible spirits other than in a dream. Hester used to come and visit me regularly. Mama Yaya, Abena, my mother, and Yao, less often. But in this case, Abigail did not have to cross the water. I was sure she could not be far away from her husband and above all from her beloved children. A few prayers and a ritual sacrifice would make her appear. And poor Benjamin's heart would be filled with joy.

About ten o'clock Benjamin joined me under a tree in blossom. He was dragging a sheep that had an immaculate coat and beautiful, submissive eyes. I had already begun my incantations and I was waiting for the moon to emerge and play its role in the ceremony. At the decisive moment I got scared, but then I felt a pair of lips on my neck and I knew it was Hester come to give me courage.

The blood of the sheep stained the earth and its pungent smell took our breath away.

After a time that seemed endless, a shape emerged and a little woman with a very white complexion and very black hair came toward us. Benjamin fell to his knees.

I discreetly moved away. Husband and wife talked for a very long time.

From then on, I allowed Benjamin Cohen d'Azevedo to see his lost, beloved wife every week. This usually occurred on Sunday evenings after the last of the friends who had come for news of the Jews scattered throughout the world had left, following a reading from their holy book. Benjamin and Abigail talked, I think, about how their business was going, about their children's education, and the trouble their youngest son, Moses, was causing them by frequenting the Gentiles and wanting to speak their language.

I say "I think" because their conversation took place in

Hebrew and I listened sort of uncomfortably to the somber sounds of that language.

After a month Benjamin asked me if he could bring his daughter Metahebel with him to these meetings.

"You cannot imagine what the death of her mother meant to her. There were only seventeen years between them and Metahebel loved Abigail like a sister. During Abigail's last days, even my love could not distinguish one from the other. They had the same laugh, the same brown plaits wound around their head, and the same perfume from their very white skins. Tituba, sometimes I start doubting God when I see him separate a child from her mother. Doubting God! You see, I am not a good Jew!"

How could I have had the heart to refuse?

Especially as Metahebel was my favorite among the children. She was so gentle that you trembled at what that inconsiderate, capricious bitch of a life could do to her. She was so attentive to others. She knew a little English and would ask me: "Why all those clouds deep in your eyes, Tituba? What are you thinking about? Your people in slavery? Don't you know that God blesses those who suffer and that's how he recognizes his own people?"

But this profession of belief did not satisfy me and I shook my head. "Metahebel, isn't it time the victims changed sides?"

From that moment on there were three of us shivering in the garden waiting for Abigail to appear. The husband and wife talked first. Then the daughter went up to her mother and they remained alone.

＊　＊　＊

Why must any relationship with the slightest hint of affection between a man and a woman necessarily end up in bed? I can't get over it.

How did Benjamin Cohen d'Azevedo, preoccupied with the memory of his dead wife, and I, with the memory of an ungrateful wretch, find ourselves involved in the act of kissing and embracing?

I believe the first time it happened he was even more surprised than I was, since he thought his penis was out of working order and was amazed to see it aroused, stiff and penetrating, swollen with seed. He was surprised and ashamed, he who taught his sons that fornication was a terrible sin. So he withdrew, stammering apologies that were swept away in another wave of desire.

Henceforth I lived in that odd situation of being both mistress and servant. The day left me with no rest. I had to card and spin the wool, wake up the children, help them wash and get dressed, make the soap, do the washing, iron, dye, weave, mend the clothing and the sheets and blankets, and even resole the shoes, not to mention making tallow for the candles, feeding the animals, and cleaning the house. For religious reasons I did not cook the meals. This was left to Metahebel and I didn't like to see her youth being wasted in household chores.

In the evening Benjamin Cohen d'Azevedo joined me in the attic, where I slept in a brass bed. I must confess that when he undressed, revealing his crooked, pasty body, I couldn't help thinking of the dark-brown muscles of John Indian. A lump would rise up in my throat and I would choke back the sobs. But that didn't last and I pitched and heaved just as well on the sea of delight with my misshapen lover. The sweetest moments, however, were those when he talked. About us. And only about us.

"Tituba, do you know what it is to be a Jew? In 629 the Merovingians expelled us from their kingdom in France. Pope Innocent III's Fourth Lateran Council ordered all Jews to wear a circular mark on their clothes and to cover their heads. Before leaving for the Crusades, Richard the Lion Hearted ordered a general attack against the Jews. Do you know how many of us lost our lives under the Inquisition?"

I retorted by interrupting him: "And what about us? Do you know how many of us have been bled from the coast of Africa?"

But he went on. "In 1298 the Jews of Rottingen were put to the sword and the wave of murders spread to Bavaria and Austria. In 1336 our blood was shed from the Rhine to Bohemia and Moravia."

He outdid me every time.

One night when we had pitched and heaved more violently than usual, Benjamin whispered passionately: "There is always a shadow at the back of your eyes, Tituba. What can I give you to make you happy or almost happy?"

"My freedom!"

The words rushed out of their own accord.

He stared at me in amazement. "Freedom? But what would you do with it?"

"I would take a berth on one of your ships and set sail immediately for my Barbados."

His face hardened and I scarcely recognized him.

"Never, never, you hear me. If you leave I'll lose her a second time. Don't ever mention it again."

And we never did mention it again. Pillow talk has the same consistency as dreams and the same peculiarity of being easily forgotten.

We resumed our old habits and gradually I settled into the ways of this Jewish family. I learned to get by in Portuguese. I became fascinated with the question of naturalization and it irritated me that the meanness of a governor should make it difficult, even impossible, to obtain citizenship. I got excited over the issue of building a synagogue and learned to think of Roger Williams as a liberal, a genuine friend of the Jews. Yes, like Benjamin Cohen d'Azevedo I began to divide the world into two groups: the friends of Jews and the others. And I began to weigh the chances the Jews might have of making a place for themselves in the New World.

One afternoon, however, I was brought back to earth. I had just taken a basket full of dried apples to Jacob Marcus's wife, who had given birth to her fourth daughter, and was crossing Front Street at a brisk pace, fighting against the wind and cold, when I heard someone call my name.

"Tituba!" It was a young Negress whom I didn't recognize at first. There were already at that time a great many blacks, whom nobody paid attention to any longer, busy doing domestic chores in the towns of Salem, Boston, and the entire Bay Colony.

Black Witch of Salem

As I hesitated, the young girl cried out: "It's me, Mary Black! Don't you remember me?"

My memory came back. Mary Black had been Nathaniel Putnam's slave. Like myself she had been accused of being a witch by the clan of little bitches and taken to Boston prison. I had no idea what had become of her.

"Mary!" All at once the past came hurtling back with its load of pain and humiliation. We sobbed in each other's arms for a few moments. Then she poured out all the news.

"The sinister scheme is now being uncovered. The girls were being manipulated by their parents. It was all a question of land, money, and old rivalries. The wind has changed now and they want to drive Samuel Parris out of the village, but he's refusing to move. He's demanding arrears in his salary and firewood that was never provided. Did you know his wife had a son?"

I didn't want to hear another word and interrupted her. "But what about you?"

She shrugged her shoulders. "I'm still at Nathaniel Putnam's. He took me back after Governor Phips's pardon. He's quarreled with his cousin Thomas. Did you know that Dr. Griggs now says that Anne Putnam and her daughter Anne were a bit out of their minds?"

Too late! Too late! The truth always arrives too late because it walks slower than lies. Truth crawls at a snail's pace. There was one question on my lips that I refrained from asking, but in the end I had to. "What has happened to John Indian?"

She hesitated and I repeated my question more insistently.

"He no longer lives in the village," she said.

I was stunned. "Where does he live then?"

"In Topsfield!"

Topsfield? I grabbed poor Mary by the arm without realizing that my fingers were digging into her innocent flesh. "Mary, for the love of God, tell me what is going on! What is he doing in Topsfield?"

She resigned herself to looking me in the face. "Do you remember Goodwife Sarah Porter?"

I, Tituba

No more than any of the others! A skinny woman whose eyes never left her prayer book at the meeting house.

"Well, he started to work for her and when her husband fell off a roof and died, he moved into her bed. There was such an outcry in the village that they had to leave."

I must have looked so distressed that she added reassuringly: "It seems that they don't get on at all."

I did not hear the rest of the conversation. It felt as though I was going mad and Hester's words came back to needle my memory: "Life is too kind to men, whatever their color."

Good for the gallows, I was wearing myself out in bondage while my man was striding around his new estate in leather boots with a conquering air and assessing his wealth. For Goody Porter was rich, I remember now. She and her late husband were among those who paid the highest taxes.

I hurried on, for the wind was sharper now, cutting through the clothes that Benjamin Cohen had given me. They still had the sweet, penetrating smell of his dead wife.

I hurried on, realizing that all I had as a refuge was the Great House in Essex Street.

When I got back, it was the hour of *Minnah*. The children were sitting around their father, saying the words that I now knew by heart. "Sh'ma Israel. Adonai Elohenu Ehad."

I ran up to my attic and let the pain flood through me.

9

But my pain passed like all the rest. It faded away and I had four months of peace, dare I say happiness, with Benjamin Cohen d'Azevedo.

At night he would murmur: "Our God knows neither race nor color. You can become one of us if you like and can pray with us."

I interrupted him with a laugh. "Your God even accepts witches?"

He kissed my hands. "Tituba, you are my beloved witch!"

At times, however, the anguish came back. I knew that misfortune never gives up. I knew it singles out those of a certain sort and I waited.

I waited.

10

It started when the mezuzahs over Benjamin Cohen d'Azeve-do's front door and over the entrances to the other two Jewish homes were ripped off and replaced by an obscene drawing in black paint.

The Jews were so used to persecution that Benjamin, sensing the situation, counted his children and herded them inside, like a docile flock. It took me hours to find Moses, who was play-ing with some street urchins near the wharf, his *kippa* hanging precariously from a lock of his thick red hair. The next day was the sabbath. As usual the five Levys and the three Marcuses slipped into Benjamin's house for the weekly ritual (Rebecca, Jacob's wife, was still at home in confinement). Hardly had their voices, which were perhaps a little shakier than usual, risen up than a hail of stones rained against the doors and windows.

Having nothing to lose, I went outside and saw a small crowd of men and women dressed in the sinister Puritan fash-ion standing some yards from the house. I was filled with rage and walked up to the aggressors.

"What are those who govern us thinking of?" one man thun-dered out. "Did we leave England for this? To see Jews and niggers multiply in our midst?"

A hail of stones rained down on me. I continued to advance, maddened with anger and light of limb. Suddenly someone shouted: "Don't you recognize her? It's Tituba, one of the witches of Salem?"

The stones flew thick and fast. They blotted out the daylight. I felt like Ti-Jean, who by willpower alone stormed the hills, pushed back the waves, and forced the sun to change its course.

I don't know how long the battle lasted. At the end of the day I woke up feeling as if every bone in my body had been broken while Metahebel in tears was changing the compresses on my forehead.

That night I had a dream. I wanted to enter a forest, but the trees were in league against me and black creepers hung down, twining themselves around me. I opened my eyes and the room was black with smoke.

In a panic I woke Benjamin Cohen d'Azevedo, who had insisted on sleeping near me to treat my wounds. He stood up and stammered: "My children!"

It was too late. The fire that had been skillfully lit at the four corners of the house had already swallowed up the first and second floors and was now licking at the attic. I had the presence of mind to throw some bedding out of the window. We landed on it in the middle of burned beams, smoldering drapes, and pieces of twisted metal. They removed nine little bodies from the ruins. Let us hope that the children, surprised in their sleep, were not frightened and did not suffer. And, after all, weren't they going to join their mother?

The town authorities granted Benjamin Cohen d'Azevedo a piece of ground to bury his children in; it became the first Jewish cemetery in the American colonies, even before the one in Newport.

As if this wasn't enough, the two ships in the port belonging to Benjamin and his friend went up in flames. Yet I do believe that this material loss left him quite indifferent. When he could find words again, Benjamin Cohen d'Azevedo came to look for me.

"There is a rational explanation for all of this. They want to bar us from the profitable trade with the West Indies. As usual, they fear and hate our ingenuity. But I have a different view. It's God who is punishing me. Not so much because of my passion for you. The Jews have always had a strong sexual instinct. Our father Moses in his great age had erections. Deuteronomy says so: 'Nor was his natural force abated.' Abraham, Jacob, and David had concubines. Neither does He begrudge me the use of your powers to see Abigail again. He recalls the love of

Abraham for Sarah. No, He is punishing me because I refused
you the only thing you desired, your freedom! Because I have
kept you with me by force, using the violence He condemns.
Because I have been selfish and cruel!"

"No, no!" I protested.

But he went on, not listening to me. "You are now free. And
here is proof."

He held out a parchment set with various seals that I didn't
even look at.

"I don't want your freedom," I said, frantically shaking my
head. "I want to stay with you."

He took me in his arms. "I am leaving for Rhode Island,
where, at least up till now, a Jew has the right to earn his living.
A Jewish friend of mine is waiting for me there."

"What will I do without you?" I sobbed.

"Go back to Barbados. Isn't that what you have always
wanted most?"

"Not at that price! Not at that price!"

"I have booked you a passage on board the ship *Bless the
Lord*, which sets sail for Bridgetown in a few days. Here is a
letter for a fellow Jew who is a merchant over there. His name
is David da Costa. I have asked him to help you, if need be."

While I was still protesting, he joined my hands in his and
made me repeat the words of Isaiah: "Thus saith the Lord, The
heaven is my throne, and the earth is my footstool: Where is the
house that ye build unto me? And where is my place of rest?"

When I was somewhat quieter, he whispered in my ear:
"I want you to grant me a last favor. Let me see my children again!"

The poor bereaved father was so impatient that we did not
wait for nightfall. Hardly had the sun set behind the bluish
roofs of Salem than we met in the orchard. I looked up at the
gnarled fingers of the trees and my heart was torn between faith
and bitterness. Metahebel appeared first, her hair adorned with
spikes of flowers like a young goddess from a pagan religion.

"Are you happy, my little treasure?" Benjamin Cohen d'Azevedo whispered.

She nodded, while her brothers and sisters sat round her.

"When will we be together?" she asked. "Make haste, father. Death is in truth the greatest fulfillment."

* * *

I was soon to find out that even armed with an act of emancipation in good and due form a Negress was not secure from delays and obstructions. The captain of the ship *Bless the Lord*, a lout by the name of Stannard, inspected me from head to toe and apparently he didn't like what he saw. While he was taking his time turning my papers over and over again in his hands, a sailor passed behind his back and whispered what he should have known already.

"Be careful, she's one of the witches of Salem!"

And here I was again, up against that epithet. I decided, however, not to let myself be intimidated and retorted: "A general pardon was decreed by the governor of the colony almost three years ago. The so-called witches have been pardoned."

"Perhaps," sneered the sailor. "But you confessed your crime so there's no pardon for you."

I was thoroughly discouraged and could find nothing to say. However, there was a cunning gleam in the wild eyes of the captain.

"Can you use magic to prevent sickness? And shipwrecks?"

I shrugged my shoulders. "I know how to heal certain sicknesses. But I can't do anything about shipwrecks."

He removed his pipe from his mouth and spat out a black, stinking saliva.

"Negress, when you speak to me, say 'Master' and lower your eyes; otherwise I'll smash those stumps out of your mouth." *

"Yes, I'll take you to Barbados, but in exchange for my goodness you will watch over the health of my crew and ward off storms."

I didn't say another word.

So he led me to the stern of the ship, cluttered with boxes of fish, casks of wine, and drums of oil, and pointed to a space between the coils of rope.

---

* I forgot to say that I had lost a good many teeth in prison.

"That's your berth!"

To tell the truth I was in no mood to go for him hammer and tongs. I could only think of the tragic events I had just been through. Mama Yaya had said it over and over again: "What matters is to survive!" But she was wrong if life is nothing but a stone around our necks. Nothing but a bitter, burning potion.

O Benjamin, my gentle, crooked lover! He had set off for Rhode Island with a prayer on his lips: "Sh'ma Israel. Adonai Elohenu Adonai Ehad!"

How many more stonings? Holocausts? How much blood had yet to be shed? How much more submission?

I began to imagine another course for life, another meaning, another motive. The fire engulfs the top of the tree. The Rebel has disappeared in a cloud of smoke. He has triumphed over death and his spirit remains. The frightened circle of slaves regains its courage. The spirit remains.

Yes, another motive for life.

In the meantime I tried to wedge my basket with its meager provisions in between the ropes, pulled the folds of my cape around me, and endeavored to savor my good fortune. Despite everything, wasn't I fulfilling the dream that had kept me awake so often? Here I was on my way to my native land.

No less rust-colored the earth. No less green the hills. No less mauve the sugarcane, sticky with juice. No less satiny the emerald belt around its waist. But the times have changed. The men and women are no longer prepared to put up with suffering. The maroon disappears in a cloud of smoke. His spirit remains. Fears fade away.

Toward the middle of the afternoon I was called out of my retreat to care for a sailor. One of the slaves working in the ship's galley was shaking with fever. He looked at me suspiciously.

"They tell me your name is Tituba. Aren't you the daughter of Abena, who killed a white man?"

Having someone recognize me after ten years of absence brought tears to my eyes. I had forgotten this ability our people have of remembering. Nothing escapes them! Everything is engraved in their memory!

"That is my name," I stammered.

His eyes filled with gentleness and respect. "I hear they gave you a difficult time over there."

How did he know? I burst into tears and through my sobs I could hear him consoling me awkwardly. "You're alive, Tituba. That's all that matters."

I shook my head violently. No, it wasn't all that mattered. Life, life had to be given a new meaning. But how?

From that moment on, the sailor, Deodatus, came to sit with me every day and secretly brought me food from the captain's table, without which I would certainly not have weathered the journey. Like Mama Yaya, he was a Nago from the Gulf of Benin. He would clasp his hands behind his neck, stare at the tangle of stars, and keep me spellbound.

"Do you know why the sky moved away from the land? A long time ago, they were very close and in the evening before they went to bed they would chatter away like old friends. But the noise of the women preparing the meals with their mortars and talking in shrill voices irritated the sky. So he withdrew higher and higher, farther and farther away behind the blue immensity above our heads."

"Do you know why the palm tree is the king of trees? Because each of its parts is essential to life. With its nuts you can make sacrificial oil, with its leaves you can cover roofs, with its fibers women can make brooms to clean the houses and compounds."

Exile, suffering, and sickness had combined in such a way as to make me almost forget these simple stories. Deodatus brought back my childhood and I never got tired of listening to him.

Sometimes he talked about his life. He had been wandering around the coast of Africa with Stannard. Some years earlier Stannard had been involved in the slave trade and Deodatus had been his interpreter. He used to accompany Stannard into the houses of the African chiefs with whom the shameful deals were made.

"Twelve slaves for a barrel of brandy, one or two pounds of gunpowder, and a silk parasol for His Majesty."

My eyes filled with tears. So much suffering for a few material goods.

"You can't imagine the greed of those African kings! They'd

sell their own subjects if laws they dare not disobey didn't forbid it! So the cruel white man steps in and takes advantage of the situation!"

We often used to talk about the future as well. Deodatus was the first to ask me outright: "What do you intend to do on the island?" Adding: "What will your freedom mean if your own people are in bondage?"

I could think of nothing in reply. For I was returning to my native land like a child running to hide in her mother's skirts.

"I'll look for my cabin on the old Darnell estate," I stammered.

"So you think it's there waiting for you," Deodatus teased. "How long is it since you've been gone?"

All these questions bothered me because I could not find answers to them. I was waiting and hoping for a sign from my invisible spirits. Alas! Nothing happened and I remained alone. Alone. For although the water of springs and rivers attracts spirits, the perpetual movement of the sea drives them away. They remain on either side of its great expanse, sometimes sending messages to those who are dear to them, but never daring to cross the waves.

"Cross the water, O my fathers! Cross the water, O my mothers!" My prayers remained unheeded.

On the fourth day Deodatus's fever, which I had cured as well as I could, spread to another member of the crew, then another and another, and we had to resign ourselves to the fact that it was an epidemic. So many fevers and sicknesses traveled between Africa, America, and the West Indies, fostered by the dirt, the promiscuity, and the bad food. There was plenty of rum, lemons from the Azores, and pepper from Cayenne on board. I administered them as scalding hot potions. I rubbed the sweating, feverish bodies with knots of straw. I did what I could and my efforts, no doubt helped by Mama Yaya, were crowned with success. Only four men died. They were thrown into the sea, who took them up in the folds of her shroud.

Do you think the captain showed any signs of gratitude . . .? On the eighth day, as the winds dropped, the water became as smooth as oil and the ship began to rock like a grandmother's rocking chair on her veranda. Stannard dragged me by my hair to the foot of the mainmast.

"Negress, if you want to save your skin, get the wind to rise! I've got perishable goods on board and if this goes on I shall have to throw them overboard, but you'll be the first to go!"

I had never dreamed I could command the elements. The man was in fact presenting me with a challenge. I turned to him and said: "I need some live animals."

Live animals? At this point in the voyage there were only a few chickens left, destined for the captain's table, a goat whose teats were swollen with milk for the captain's breakfast, and a few cats thrown in to hunt the mice on board. They were duly brought to me.

Milk! Blood! Didn't I have the essential liquids plus the docile flesh of the sacrificial victims?

I stared at the sea; it was like a forest that had burned to the ground.

Suddenly, a bird emerged from the motionless cinders and rose straight up into the sun. Then it stopped, wheeled in a circle, then hovered again before soaring upward. I knew it was a sign and that the prayers in my heart would not remain unanswered.

The bird was now no more than a tiny speck disappearing into the sky and for a time the world was suspended, waiting for a mysterious decision. Then a great whistling from one of the corners of the horizon filled the air. The sky changed color, from a violent blue to a sort of very soft gray. The sea started to be flecked with white and a funnel of wind whirled round the sails, tangling them up, undoing the ropes, and breaking in two a mast that collapsed, killing a sailor. I realized that my sacrifices had not been enough and that the spirits were also demanding *a sheep without horns*. At dawn on the sixteenth day we arrived in sight of Barbados. I looked for Deodatus when we arrived, to say good-bye, but he had disappeared in the confusion. I felt an aching void.

11

My sweet, crooked, misshapen lover! Before losing you forever I can remember our meager moments of happiness together. When you joined me in my big bed in the attic, we used to pitch and plunge like a drunken boat on a choppy sea. We rowed together under your guidance and finally reached the shore. Sleep washed us softly up on the beach and in the morning we could start our daily chores refreshed. My sweet, crooked, misshapen lover! We did not make love the last night we spent together, as if our souls were taking over from our bodies. Once again, you blamed yourself for your hardness. And once again I begged you to leave me my chains.

Hester, Hester, you would be angry with me. But some men who have the virtue of being weak instill in us the desire to be a slave!

12

The invisible trio was there among the crowd of slaves, sailors, and idlers come to welcome me. Spirits have that particularity of never getting old and keeping their youthful features forever. Mama Yaya, the tall Nago Negress with sparkling teeth. Abena, my mother, the Ashanti princess with her jet-black skin and ritual scarifications. Yao, the silk-cotton tree with large, powerful feet.

I cannot describe my feelings while they hugged me.

Apart from that, my island did not exactly deck itself out to greet me. It was raining in Bridgetown and the flock of wet tiled roofs was huddled around the massive silhouette of its cathedral. The streets were churned with muddy water in which men and beasts were splashing. It looked as though a slave ship had just anchored because a group of English men and women were inspecting the teeth, tongue, and genitals, of the *bossales*, who were shaking with humiliation under a thatched market awning.

How ugly my town was! Small. Petty. A colonial outpost of no distinction, reeking with the stench of lucre and suffering.

I walked up Broad Street and almost unintentionally found myself in front of the house of my old enemy, Susanna Endicott. But instead of rejoicing when Mama Yaya whispered in my ear how the shrew had given up the ghost after having marinated for weeks in her stinging urine, I was overtaken by a sudden emotion.

What wouldn't I have given to relive those years when I slept night after night in the arms of my John Indian, with my hand on his pleasure-dispensing object! What wouldn't I have given to see him standing under the low door and greeting me in that ironic and tender way he was so good at.

"Well, there you are my poor, suffering wife! You've been through life like a rolling stone and here you are back, empty-handed!"

I tried to swallow back the tears, but they did not escape Abena, my mother, who sighed: "Well I never! She's crying for that wretch!"

After this note of discord, the three spirits rolled themselves into a translucent cloud that rose above the houses and Mama Yaya explained: "Someone is calling us. We'll see you tonight."

"Don't let yourself be waylaid," Abena, my mother, added. "Go home!"

Home! There was a cruel irony in this word. Apart from a handful of dead people, nobody was waiting for me on this island and I didn't even know whether the cabin I had squatted in ten years earlier was still standing. If not, I would have to turn myself into a carpenter again and build myself a shelter somewhere. The prospects were so uninviting that I was tempted to go and find this David da Costa for whom Benjamin Cohen d'Azevedo had given me a letter . . . Where did he live?

I was hesitating on which way to turn when I saw a group of individuals wading through the mud toward me, covering themselves as best they could with banana leaves. I recognized Deodatus in between two women and I cried out in joy: "Where were you? I've been looking for you everywhere."

He smiled mysteriously.

"I went and told a few friends you'd arrived. I knew they would be delighted."

One of the young women then curtsied in front of me. "Honor us, mother, with your presence."

Mother? The word made me jump and boil with rage, since it was a term of respect reserved for old women. I was hardly thirty and less than a month ago the hot seed of a man was being spilled on my thighs. Hiding my discontent, I took Deodatus's arm and asked: "And where do your friends live?"

"Near Belleplaine."

"Belleplaine!" I almost shouted. "That's at the other end of the island!"

But I pulled myself together. Hadn't I just been thinking that nobody was waiting for me and that I had no roof over my head? So why not Belleplaine?

We left the town and suddenly, as is often the case in our islands, the rain stopped and the sun started to shine again, brushing the contours of the hills with light. The sugarcane was in flower, like a purple cloud above the fields. The shiny green leaves of the yams were mounting an attack on their poles. A feeling of lightness drove out my previous thoughts. How could I have believed that nobody was waiting for me when the whole island was there for me to behold lovingly? Wasn't Zenaida the bird warbling for me? Weren't the pawpaw, orange, and pomegranate trees loaded with fruit for me?

Heartened, I turned to Deodatus, who was walking beside me, respecting my silence, and asked: "But who are your friends? What plantation do they work on?"

He gave a little laugh, which the two women echoed. "They don't work on any plantation."

For a moment I didn't understand, then I asked unbelievingly: "They don't work on a plantation? Then they must be . . . maroons?"

Deodatus nodded.

Maroons? Ten years earlier, when I had left Barbados, maroons were few and far between. There was merely talk of a certain Ti-Noel and his family, who held Farley Hill. Nobody had ever seen him. He had been living in everyone's imagination for so long that he must have been an old man by now. Yet he was said to be young and bold and his exploits had become household legends: "The white man's gun cannot kill Ti-Noel. His dog cannot bite him. His fire cannot burn him. Open up the gate, Papa Ti-Noel."

"My friends took to the hills some years ago when the French attacked the island," Deodatus explained. "The English then wanted to enroll the slaves by force into an army as a means of defense. But the slaves replied: 'What! Me die for a white man's quarrel!' and they ran off as fast as their legs would carry them. They hid in Chalky Mountain and the English still can't smoke them out."

Again the women laughed in unison.

I didn't know what to think. Despite all I had just been through and this unfulfilled lust for revenge inside me, I hadn't the heart to get involved with maroons and to risk my life for them. Paradoxically, I realized that all I wanted was to live in peace on my island regained. So the rest of the journey was made in silence.

When the sun was already high in the sky, the women motioned to us to stop and pulled some fruit and dried meat out of their bags. We shared this frugal meal, which Deodatus washed down with rum. Then we set off again. The road became steeper and steeper while the vegetation became profuse and luxuriant as if it too were intent on protecting the outlaws. At a certain moment the women said out loud, "Ago."

The bushes parted and three men emerged, armed with guns. They greeted us warmly, but nonetheless blindfolded us and we entered the maroon camp in total darkness.

*   *   *

The maroons listened to me as they sat in a circle. There weren't very many, not more than fifteen with their wives and children. And I relived my suffering, my hearing before the tribunal, the unfounded accusations, the false confessions, and the betrayal by those I loved. When I had finished, they all started speaking at once.

"How many times did you meet this Satan?"

"Is he more powerful than the greatest of our obeah men?"

"Did he make you write in his book and do you know how to write?"

Christopher, their leader, a man of about forty, as peaceful as those rivers that flow inexorably toward the sea, stopped them with his hand and said apologetically: "You must excuse them, they are warriors not *grangreks* and they have not understood that you were being accused wrongly. For you were innocent, weren't you?"

I nodded.

"You have no secret powers?" he insisted.

I don't know what came over me. Vanity? A desire to arouse a keener interest in the eyes of this man? A craving for sincerity? Anyway I tried to explain. "The woman who brought me up, a Nago, left me some secret powers. But I only use them to do good . . ."

The maroons interrupted me in unison. "Do good? Even to your enemies?"

I didn't know what to say. Fortunately, Christopher gave the signal to retire for the night. Getting up he yawned: "Tomorrow is another day."

I had been given a hut not far from the one he occupied with his two concubines, for he had reinstated to his advantage the African custom of polygamy. It seemed as though I had never slept on a softer mattress than this straw bedding placed on the earth floor under the thatched roof. Ah yes, life had pushed me around! From Salem to Ipswich. From Barbados to America and back. But now I could sit down and rest and say: "You won't manhandle me anymore!"

The rain started up again and I could hear it pitter-patter like an exasperated visitor who is kept waiting at the door.

I was about to sink into sleep when I heard a noise at the entrance to the hut. I was thinking it must be my invisible spirits come to reproach me for having forgotten about them when Christopher entered, holding a candle above his head. I sat up.

"What's the matter? Aren't your two wives enough for you?"

He rolled his eyes and I was immediately mortified at what I had said. "Listen, I'm in no mood for sexual banter," he replied.

"What are you in the mood for?" I asked flirtatiously, as despite all my misfortunes, I had not lost that deep instinct that makes me a woman.

He sat down on a stool and set his candle on the ground so that it made a thousand flickering shadows. "I want to know if I can count on you."

For a moment I remained speechless, then said: "For what, in heaven's name?"

He leaned toward me. "Do you remember the song about Ti-Noel?"

Ti-Noel? I gave up trying to understand.

He stared at me with a look of commiseration as if I were a dull-witted child and started to sing in a surprisingly good voice.

" 'Oh, Papa Ti-Noel, the white man's gun cannot kill him. The white man's bullets cannot kill him. They bounce off his skin.' Tituba, I want you to make me invincible."

So that was it. I almost burst out laughing, but refrained for fear of irritating him, and managed to reply very calmly: "I don't know whether I'm capable of that, Christopher!"

"Are you a witch?" he shouted. "Yes or no!"

I sighed. "Everyone gives that word a different meaning. Everyone believes he can fashion a witch to his way of thinking so that she will satisfy his ambitions, dreams, and desires . . ."

"Listen," he interrupted. "I'm not going to stay here listening to you philosophize! I'm offering you a deal. You make me invincible and in exchange . . ."

"In exchange?"

He got up and his head almost touched the ceiling while his shadow loomed over me like a guardian spirit.

"In exchange I'll give you everything a woman desires."

"Meaning what?" I said ironically.

He did not answer and turned on his heels. He had hardly left the room when I heard sighs that I recognized immediately. I decide to ignore Abena, my mother, and turned to the wall, calling on Mama Yaya.

"Can I help him?"

Mama Yaya puffed on her small pipe and sent a smoke ring into the air.

"How could you? Death is a door that nobody can lock. Everybody has to go through it when his day and hour come. You know full well it can only be kept open for those we love so that they can catch a glimpse of those they left behind."

"Can't I try to help him?" I insisted. "He's fighting for a noble cause."

Abena, my mother, burst out laughing. "Hypocrite! Is it the cause he's fighting for that interests you? Come now!"

I closed my eyes in the dark. The formidable perspicacity of my mother irritated me. In addition, I reprimanded myself. Hadn't I had enough of men? Hadn't I had enough of the misfortune that goes with their affections? Hardly was I back in Barbados than I was contemplating a life of adventure with no idea of how it would end. A band of maroons whom I knew nothing about. I promised myself I would ask Deodatus about his friends and then I slowly sank into sleep.

Great white water lilies wrapped me in their brocade petals and soon Hester, Metahebel, and my Jew came and sat around my bed. My affection and my nostalgia confused the living with the dead.

My Jew seemed reassured, almost happy, as if over there in Rhode Island he was at least allowed to worship his God in peace.

At one moment the rain fell in soft whispers, drenching plants, trees, and roofs, unlike the hostile, icy rains I recalled in the land I had left behind. Yes, nature changes her language according to the land, and curiously, her language harmonizes with that of man. Savage nature, savage men! Protecting, well-meaning nature, openhearted and generous men!

My first night on my island!

The croaking of the frogs and agua toads, the trill of the night birds, the cackling of the chickens frightened by the mongooses, and the braying of the donkeys tied to the calabash trees, the spirit's resting place, kept up a continual music. I never wanted the morning to come. I never wanted to wake up. I fleetingly recalled my days in Boston and Salem, but they lost all consistency, like those who had blackened them with the venom of their hearts—Samuel Parris and the others.

My first night!

The island is alive with a soft murmur. "She is back. She is here, the daughter of Abena, the daughter of Mama Yaya. She will never leave us again."

13

I had never thought of surpassing Mama Yaya in magic powers.
I had never even thought of acting without her guidance. I had
always considered myself her child, her pupil. Alas! I have to
confess to my shame that my way of thinking changed and the
pupil got it into her head to rival the master. After all, I did
have reason to be proud. Hadn't I commanded the elements on
board the ship *Bless the Lord?* There was nothing to prove that
I did it with outside help. I now devoted my time to experi-
ments of my own making, roaming the countryside armed with
a large bag and a small knife for digging up herbs. Likewise, I
endeavored to strike up a new conversation with the rivers and
the wind, in order to discover their secrets.

The river runs toward the sea like life running toward death
and nothing can stop its course. Why?

Why does the wind sometimes caress and sometimes destroy?

I increased the number of sacrifices of fresh fruit, food, and
live animals that I laid at crossroads, in the tangled roots of
certain trees, and in the natural grottoes where spirits like to
hide. Since Mama Yaya did not want to help me, all I had to
count on was my intelligence and my intuition. I had to arrive
at this higher sphere of knowledge on my own. I therefore set
about making inquiries among the slaves concerning the obeah
men and women who lived on the plantations and then I went
visiting them. I was greeted with enormous mistrust. Obeah
men and women, you know, do not like sharing their science
and are like cooks who never want to give away a recipe.

One day I came across an obeah man, an Ashanti like Abena,
my mother, who started to tell me the story of his capture off

Akwapim on the coast of Africa. His wife, who was an Ashanti as well, slaves preferring to form couples by "nation," was peeling tubers for their dinner. Then he said in a vague kind of way: "Where do you live?"

"On the other side of the hills," I stammered, as I had been told not to reveal the site of the maroon camp.

"Aren't you Tituba?" he snorted. "The one white folks almost had swinging on the end of a rope?"

I answered in my usual way. "I was beyond reproach, you know."

"A pity! A pity!"

I stared at him, speechless.

"If I had been in your shoes," he went on, "ah! I would have bewitched every one of them: mothers, fathers, children, and neighbors. . . . I would have turned them one against the other and I would have delighted in watching them tear one another to pieces. There wouldn't have been just a hundred people accused and twenty executed. The whole of Massachusetts would have been hanged and I would have gone down in history as the demon of Salem. Whereas what name do you have?"

I was mortified by his words, because such thoughts had already crossed my mind. I had already regretted having played only a minor role in the whole affair and having had a fate that no one could remember. "Tituba, a slave originating from the West Indies and probably practicing 'hoodoo.'" A few lines in the many volumes written on the Salem witch trials. Why was I going to be ignored? This question too had crossed my mind. Is it because nobody cares about a Negress and her trials and tribulations? Is that why?

I can look for my story among those of the witches of Salem, but it isn't there. In August 1706 Anne Putnam stood up in the middle of the church in Salem and confessed the errors of her childhood, regretting their terrible consequences: "I desire to lie in the dust and earnestly beg forgiveness of all those unto whom I have given just cause of sorrow and offense and whose relations were taken away and accused."

She was neither the first nor the last to confess publicly,

and one by one the victims were rehabilitated. But not a word about me. "Tituba, a slave originating from the West Indies and probably practicing 'hoodoo.'"

I lowered my head and didn't answer. As if he could read my mind and did not want to upset me further, the obeah man softened his tone. "Life isn't always a bowl of arrowroot, is it?"

I got up, ignoring the pity in his remark. "Dusk is falling and I have to go home."

A cunning gleam erased his fleeting look of sympathy. "What you have in mind is impossible," he said. "Are you forgetting that you're in the land of the living?"

I set off back to the maroon camp, turning his final words over and over in my mind. Did he mean that only death brings supreme knowledge? That while you are alive there's a boundary you cannot cross? That I would have to resign myself to partial knowledge?

As I was about to leave the plantation, a group of slaves came up to me. I thought they needed treatment, women asking for potions, children needing compresses for their wounds, or men showing me their limbs crushed by the mills, for my knowledge of plants had rapidly given me a reputation all over the island and the sick would come up to me as soon as I appeared.

But this was another affair all together.

"Be careful, mother!" the slaves cried out with long faces. "The planters got together yesterday evening and they are after your skin."

I couldn't believe it. What crime could they accuse me of? What had I done since I arrived but treat the neglected?

A man explained: "They say you've been carrying messages between the field hands, helping them to plan revolts, and so they're going to set a trap for you."

I set off back to the camp in dismay.

Those of you who have read my tale up till now must be wondering who is this witch devoid of hatred, who is mislead each time by the wickedness in men's hearts? For the nth time I made up my mind to be different and fight it out tooth and nail. But how to work a change in my heart and coat its lining with snake venom? How to make it into a vessel for bitter and violent feelings? To get it to love evil? Instead, I could only feel tenderness and compassion for the disinherited and a sense of revolt against injustice.

The sun was setting behind Farley Hill. The insects of the night were starting up their persistent trill. The ragged group of slaves was returning to their sugarcane alleys while the overseers were spurring their horses home with the prospect of drinking a glass of neat rum and rocking in a chair on their veranda. On seeing me they cracked their whips as if they were eager to use them on me. But none of them dared do so.

I reached the camp at nightfall.

Underneath the thick ring of silk-cotton trees the women were roasting over an open fire slabs of meat they had basted with lemon and hot peppers mixed with bay-rum leaves. Christopher's two concubines scowled at me, wondering what was going on between their man and me. Previously I had been touched by their tender age and I had sworn never to do anything that would hurt them. That evening, however, I didn't even look at them.

Christopher was in his hut rolling a cigar with the tobacco leaves that grew so well on the island and from which certain planters were making a fortune.

"Where have you been roaming all day long?" he gibed. "Is that how you expect to find the remedy I asked you for?"

I shrugged my shoulders. "I have inquired of people far more knowledgeable than I and they all say there is no remedy against death. Rich man, poor man, slave and master—there is no escaping it. But listen, things have got to change. Let me fight the white folks with you."

He threw back his head and laughed, the echoes of his laughter mixing with the curls of smoke from his cigar.

"Fight? You're going too fast. A woman's duty, Tituba, is not to fight or make war, but to make love!"

* * *

The next few weeks went by in perfect happiness. Despite the slaves' warnings, I still went down to the plantations. I now chose the hour after sunset, the hour when the spirits take possession of the air. Although they were unhappy at my taking up residence at Farley Hill, Mama Yaya and Abena, my mother, nevertheless visited me each day and accompanied me along the rough, winding paths through the fields. I paid no heed to their grumblings.

"What are you doing living with those maroons? They're bad people who spend their time killing and stealing!"

"They're just a bunch of ungrateful wretches who leave their mothers and brothers in slavery while they themselves live a life of freedom."

What was the point of arguing?

It was during these weeks that I experienced a wonderful moment of happiness. I brought back to life a little baby girl who was hardly out of her mother's womb. She hadn't yet stepped through death's door and was hesitating in that dark corridor preparing for her departure. I held the little thing back. She was warm and covered in mucus and excrement and I laid her softly on her mother's breast. You should have seen the expression on that woman's face! How mysterious motherhood is!

For the first time I asked myself whether my child, whose life I had taken, would not after all have given my existence a meaning and a purpose.

Hester, did we make a mistake and shouldn't you have lived for your child instead of dying with her?

Christopher had got into the habit of spending the night in my hut. I don't quite know how this new adventure began. A lingering look, kindling the flames of desire? The will to prove to myself that I was not yet finished or dispensed with like a worn-out beast of burden? Yet need I say it, this commerce only involved my senses. All the rest of me continued to belong to John Indian, whom, paradoxically, I thought about more and more each day.

My man, full of hot air and bravado, as Mama Yaya used to say. My treacherous, weakhearted man!

While Christopher was writhing on top of me, my mind would roam and I would relive the pleasures of my nights in America. Listen to the howl of winter as it galloped in the night over the frost-covered ground. We were oblivious to everything, John Indian and I, as we suffocated in love. Samuel Parris, buttoned up in black from head to foot, would be reciting his prayers. Listen to his stony dirge: "But mine enemies are lively and they are strong and they that hate me wrongfully are multiplied."

John Indian and I were oblivious to everything as we succumbed to love.

Gradually Christopher, who had possessed my body in silence, began to confide in me. "There are not enough of us and there are too few arms to attack the white folks. All we have is half a dozen guns and a few wooden cudgels. We live with the constant fear of being attacked. And that's the truth of the matter."

"Is that why you want me to make you invincible?" I asked, a little disappointed.

He reacted to the mockery in my voice and turned toward the wall. "What does it matter if you do or you don't. In any case I shall be immortal. I've already heard the field niggers singing."

And, in his pleasant voice, he sang a song of his own composition, boasting of his merits.

I touched him on the shoulder. "And what about me, is there a song for me? A song for Tituba?"

He pretended to listen hard, then said: "No, there isn't!" Thereupon he began to snore and I tried to do the same.

When I was not treating the slaves on the plantations I helped the maroon women. At first they had treated me with the greatest respect. Then when they learned that Christopher shared my bed and that, after all, I was no different from them, they became antagonistic. This hostility had now given way to an expression of sullen solidarity. After all, they needed me. One would ask me to fill her withered breast with milk. Another to treat the pain she had had since last giving birth. I listened to them chatter, finding amusement, relaxation, and pleasure in their conversations.

"A long, long time ago when the devil was still a little boy in white drill shorts stiffened with starch, the world was inhabited only by women. They worked together, slept together, and bathed together in the river. One day one of them called the others together and said: 'Sisters, when we go, who will replace us? We haven't created a single person in our image.' The others shrugged their shoulders: 'Why do we need to be replaced?' But some of them thought they should be. 'For who will farm the land without us? It will lie fallow and fruitless.' So they all started to look for ways of reproducing themselves and that's how they invented man!"

We all laughed together.

"Why are men as they are?"

"If only we knew, my dear!"

Sometimes they asked each other riddles. "What cures the darkness of the night?" "The candle!" "What cures the heat of the day?" "The water from the river!" "What cures the bitterness of life?" "A child!"

And they would pity me for never having had a child. And then, moving from one thing to another, they would press me with questions. "When the judges of Salem sent you to prison, couldn't you have turned yourself into a mouse, for example, and disappeared between two loose boards in the floor? Or an angry bull and gored them all with your horns?"

I shrugged my shoulders and once again I explained they were mistaken and were exaggerating the extent of my powers.

One evening the discussion went farther and I had to defend myself. "If I could do everything, wouldn't I have set you free? Wouldn't I have wiped away the wrinkles on your faces? And replaced the stumps in your gums by gleaming, pearly white teeth?"

Their faces remained skeptical and, discouraged, I said with a shrug: "Believe me, I'm just a poor creature!"

Were my words commented upon? Distorted or misinterpreted? In any case, Christopher started to change toward me. He would come into my hut in the middle of the night and take me without removing his clothes. This reminded me of Elizabeth Parris's complaint: "My poor Tituba, he takes me without either removing his clothes or looking at me."

When I tried to ask him how he had spent his day, he would answer irritably in monosyllables.

"They say you're organizing a general revolt with the slaves in Saint James."

"Woman, hold your tongue!"

"They say you've obtained a batch of guns with a surprise attack on an ammunitions depot in Wildey?"

"Woman, can't you leave me in peace!"

One evening he blurted out: "You're nothing but a common Negress, but you want to be treated like someone special!"

I knew then that I had to go and that my presence was no longer wanted.

Just before dawn I called on Mama Yaya and Abena, my mother, who for some days now had kept away as if they were refusing to witness my downfall. I had to beg them to come and when they appeared, filling the hut with their perfume of guava and rosewood, they stared at me reproachfully.

"Your hair is already turning gray and you still can't do without men!"

I didn't answer. After a while I decided to look them straight in the face. "I'm going home!"

Strangely enough, as soon as the women heard I was leaving they gathered round looking distressed. One gave me a carefully trussed chicken, another some fruit, and yet another, a black-and-brown-checkered madras headcloth. They accompanied me to the hedge of *rayo* trees, while Christopher, who pretended to be holding counsel with his men in his hut, did not even take the trouble to appear on the doorstep.

* * *

I found my cabin very much as I had left it. Just a little more crooked. Just a little more worm-eaten under a roof that looked like an untidy mop of hair. A poinsettia was bleeding by a window. Some banana quits, which had nested between two planks devoured by termites, flew out with plaintive cries. I opened the door wide and some surprised rats scampered out.

The slaves, who somehow knew of my return, welcomed me home. The plantation had once again changed hands. It had first belonged to an absentee planter who was merely content to repatriate his profits which were never up to his expectations. Now it had just been bought by a certain Errin, who had brought out some sophisticated machinery from England and intended to make a fortune as quickly as possible.

The slaves brought me a ewe that had a triangle of black hair on its forehead as if it were predestined. They had picked up enough courage to remove it from their master's flock.

I sacrificed the animal shortly before dawn and let its blood soak into the scarlet-colored earth. After that I set to work. I built up a garden of all the herbs I needed to practice my art, boldly descending into the wildest, most secluded valleys. At the same time I laid out a kitchen garden that the slaves helped me to dig, hoe, and weed once their day's labor was over. One of them would manage to bring me some okra and tomato seeds, another a lemon tree cutting. Several of the slaves set to work planting yams and soon the avid creepers could be seen twining around their poles. Once I had got together a few hens and a strutting, fighting cock, nothing was missing.

My working day was very simple. I got up at dawn, prayed, went down to bathe in the River Ormond, had a bite to eat, then spent my time on my explorations and healing. At that time cholera and smallpox struck the plantations regularly and laid to rest a good many of the slaves. I discovered how to treat these illnesses. I also discovered how to treat yaws and to heal those wounds the slaves got day after day. I managed to mend open, festering wounds, to put pieces of bone back together again, and to tie up limbs. All that, of course, with the help of my invisible spirits, who hardly ever left me. I had given up the illusion of making men invincible and immortal. I accepted the limits of the species.

The reader may be surprised that at a time when the lash was constantly being used, I managed to enjoy this peace and freedom. Our islands have two sides to them. The side of the masters' carriages and their constables on horseback, armed with muskets and savage, baying hounds. And the other, mysterious, and secret side, composed of passwords, whispers, and a conspiracy of silence. It was on this side that I lived, protected by common collusion. Mama Yaya made a thick vegetation grow up around my cabin and it was as if I lived in a fortified castle. An inexperienced eye could only make out a tangle of guava trees, ferns, frangipani, and acoma trees, specked here and there by the mauve flower of a hibiscus.

One day I discovered an orchid among the mossy roots of a fern and I named it Hester.

14

A few weeks after I had returned home, dividing my time between my herbs and healing the slaves, I realized I was pregnant. Pregnant!

To start with, I couldn't believe it. Wasn't I an old woman
with flat, withered breasts hanging over my rib cage and rolls
of fat over my belly? Nevertheless I had to face facts. Christopher's brutal embraces had conceived what the love of my Jew
had not been able to do. You've got to face up to it. A child in
fact is not the fruit of love but of chance.

When I told Mama Yaya and Abena, my mother, about my
condition, they remained evasive, simply commenting: "Well,
this time you can't do away with it!"

"Your real nature has spoken!"

I attributed this reserve to their dislike of Christopher. I now
had time only for myself. Because once the initial moments
of doubt and uncertainty were over, I let myself be carried
away, rolled, and immersed in a great wave of happiness and
intoxication. Everything I did now revolved around this life I
carried inside me. I kept myself fed on fresh fruit, milk from
a white goat, and eggs laid by hens nourished with grains of
corn. I bathed my eyes in a decoction of cochlearia so that the
little being would have good eyesight. I washed my hair with
the cream of palma christi oil seeds so that its own would be
black and shiny. I took long, drowsy siestas in the shade of the
mango trees. And yet my child made me combative. I was sure
it was a girl! What sort of life was in store for her? That of
my brothers and sisters, the slaves, ruined by their conditions
and their labor? Or a life like mine, which forced me to live
in hiding as an outcast and a recluse on the edge of a secluded
valley?

No, if the world were going to receive my child, then it would have to change!

At one stage I was tempted to return to Farley Hill, not to inform Christopher of my condition (he didn't care one bit), but to try and urge him to do something. I knew that a good many planters were discouraged by the size of our island and were leaving to seek bigger lands that suited their ambitions better. They were leaving in particular for Jamaica, which the English army had just captured from the Spanish. Who knows, by starting a reign of terror we might be able to precipitate their departure and kick them all into the sea. Very quickly, however, I recalled his confession of weakness, even more than his inglorious behavior toward me. I made up my mind to count on no one but myself. But how?

I increased the number of prayers and sacrifices, hoping that the invisible world would give me a sign. Nothing of the sort happened. I tried to ask Mama Yaya and Abena, my mother. I tried to catch them off guard and get them to tell me what they thought it was their duty to hide from me. To no avail. The two wily old birds always managed to turn a pirouette and elude the point.

"He who wants to know why the sea is so blue finds himself lying under the waves."

"The sun burns the wings of the braggart who tries to get too close."

That was how things stood when the slaves brought me a boy whom the overseer's lash had left for dead. He had received 250 whiplashes on his legs, buttocks, and back, and his body, weakened by a spell in prison, had collapsed. The boy was a hardened offender and nobody could tame his insolence. The slaves were carrying him to an unmarked grave in a field of Guinea grass when they noticed that he was still alive. They then decided to hand him over to me.

I laid Iphigene (for that was his name) on a straw mattress in a corner of my bedroom so that I could hear his every murmur. I prepared poultices and plasters for his wounds. On those that were infected I placed a fresh slice of animal liver so that it would absorb the pus and the bad blood. I kept renewing the compresses on his forehead and went down to the bottom of

Codrington Valley to collect the spit of the agua toad. This was the only place where the toad could be found, because of its liking for the rich brown soil. After twenty-four hours of constant attention, I was rewarded, and Iphigene opened his eyes. On the third day he spoke. "Mother, O mother, you've come back! I thought you had gone forever!"

I took his hand that was still hot with fever and already rough and distorted. "I'm not your mother, Iphigene. But I'd like you to tell me about her."

Iphigene opened his eyes wider, realized his mistake, and lay back down on the bedding in pain.

"I saw my mother die when I was three. She was one of Ti-Noel's women, for he had a great many scattered throughout the plantations to reproduce his seed. His virile seed, from which I came. My mother brought me up with devotion. Alas! She had the misfortune to be beautiful. One day she was coming back from the mill when the master, Edward Dashby, noticed her. Despite her rags and sweat, he ordered the overseer to bring her to him at nightfall. Nobody knows what happened exactly, but the next morning she was whipped to death in front of a circle of slaves."

How like my own story! At once, the affection I had immediately felt for Iphigene blossomed, finding, so to speak, a legitimate reason. In turn, I recounted my life, bits of which he already knew, since I had become a legend among the slaves, far more than I could possibly have imagined.

When I got to the burning of Benjamin Cohen d'Azevedo's house, he interrupted me with a frown: "But why? Wasn't he white like the others?"

"No doubt."

"Do they need to hate so much that they hate each other?"

I tried to explain what I remembered from Benjamin's and Metahebel's lessons concerning their religion and their quarrels with the Gentiles. But Iphigene didn't understand any more than I did.

Gradually, Iphigene managed to sit up in bed and then to stand. Soon he was taking a few steps outside. His first job was to repair the front door, which didn't close properly.

Black Witch of Salem

"Mother, you need a man about the house!" he said, preening himself.

I could hardly keep myself from laughing out loud, he said it so seriously. What a handsome young man Iphigene was! He had a perfectly oval head under tight, pepper-grain hair. High cheekbones. His purple, pulpy lips seemed to want to kiss the whole world if only it would let itself be kissed instead of constantly spurning and rejecting! The lashes that had scarred his chest and torso were constant reminders of this cruelty. Every time I rubbed him with palma christi balm, my heart would swell in anger and revolt.

One morning I could hold back no longer. "Iphigene, you've probably noticed that I'm with child?"

He lowered his eyes discreetly. "I didn't dare mention it."

"Listen, I dream of bringing my daughter into a different world."

He remained silent for a moment, as if he were taking stock of my words. Then he rushed over to me and kneeled down at my feet in his favorite position. "Mother, I know by name and by plantation all those who would follow you. We only have to say the word."

"We haven't got any weapons."

"We've got fire. Magnificent fire that devours and burns!"

"What will we do once we've kicked them into the sea? Who will govern?"

"Mother, the white folks really went to work on you! You think too much! Let's drive them out first!"

In the afternoon when I came back from my daily bath in the River Ormond, I found Iphigene deep in conversation with two young boys of his own age, two *bossales*, who I thought were Nagos. But I didn't recognize the sounds of Mama Yaya's language and Iphigene told me they were Mandingos from a mountainous region and were used to all the tricks of the forest.

"They're real war chiefs. Prepared to win or die."

I must admit that once we had both agreed on the idea of a general revolt, Iphigene no longer consulted me on anything. I let him do what he wanted while I drifted lazily into the delights of pregnancy, caressing my belly that grew rounder under my touch and singing songs to my baby. There was an air that Abena, my mother, used to hum and now it came back to me:

> Up there in the woods,
> There's an *ajoupa*,
> Nobody knows who's inside.
> Nobody knows who lives there.
> It's a *calenda* zombie
> Who's fond of fat pigs.

It wasn't long before I saw Iphigene stacking torches made of guava wood and tipped with tow.

"Each of our men will be holding one," he explained. "He will light it and at the same time, in a single move, we will march on the Great Houses. What a wonderful bonfire it will be!"

I lowered my head and said in a distressed tone of voice: "The children, too, will die? Babies at their mothers' breast? Children with milk teeth? And young marriageable girls?"

He spun round in anger. "You told me yourself they had no pity for Dorcas Good or for the children of Benjamin Cohen d'Azevedo."

I lowered my head farther and murmured: "Do we have to become like them?"

He strode off without saying a word. I called Mama Yaya, who was sitting cross-legged on the branch of a calabash tree.

"You know what we are doing," I said excitedly. "But now that the time has come to act, I remember what you told me when I wanted to take my revenge on Susanna Endicott: 'Don't pervert your heart! Don't become like them!' Is this the price to pay for freedom?"

But instead of giving me the serious answer I was counting on, Mama Yaya began to hop from branch to branch. When she had reached the top of the tree she cried out: "You talk about freedom. Have you any idea what it means?"

Then she disappeared before I had time to ask her any more questions. I took it that she was in a bad mood. Did she have to find fault with every man who lived with me? Even if he were but a child. Why did she want me to live in solitude? I made up my mind to do without her advice and to let Iphigene do as he pleased.

One evening he came and sat down beside me. "Mother, you've got to return to the maroon camp to see Christopher."

I jumped up. "Never! I'll never do that!"

"You must!" he insisted, firmly but respectfully. "You don't realize what the maroons actually represent. There is a tacit agreement between them and the planters. And if they want the planters to let them enjoy their precarious freedom, they have to denounce every plot and every attempt at a slave revolt they hear about on the island. So they have their spies everywhere. Only you can disarm Christopher."

I shrugged my shoulders. "Do you really believe I can?"

"Isn't that his child you're carrying?" he asked, embarrassed. I didn't answer. However, I realized he was right and set off for Farley Hill.

*   *   *

"Did he promise he wouldn't interfere?"

"He promised."

"Did he seem sincere?"

"As far as I could judge! After all I don't know him very well."

"You're carrying his child and you say you don't know him very well?"

Humiliated, I didn't say a word. Iphigene got up.

"We've decided to attack in four nights' time!"

"In four nights' time!" I protested. "Why in such a hurry? Let me at least ask the spirits if the time is right."

He laughed, echoed by his fellow maroons. "Up till now the spirits haven't treated you so well. Otherwise you wouldn't be where you are today. The time is right because the moon will be in its fourth quarter and will not rise before midnight. Our men will have darkness on their side. They will sound the conch in unison and then with lighted torch in hand they will march on the Great Houses."

*   *   *

That night I had a dream.

Three men came into my room like three great birds of prey.

They were wearing black hoods over their faces and yet I knew it was Samuel Parris, John Indian, and Christopher. They came up to me holding a thick, sharpened stick and I screamed: "No, no! Haven't I already gone through that?"

Without heeding my cries, they lifted up my skirts and I was racked with a terrible pain. I screamed even louder.

At that moment someone laid a hand on my forehead. It was Iphigene. I came to and sat up, terrified, thinking I was still suffering.

"What's the matter? Don't be afraid, I'm here by your side."

My dream was so vivid that I remained speechless for a while, reliving the horrible night before my arrest.

"Iphigene," I begged, "give me time to pray, to make a sacrifice and try to reconcile the unseen forces . . ."

"Tituba," he interrupted (and this was the first time he had called me by my name, as if I were no longer his mother but a naive, unreasonable child), "I respect your talents as a healer. Isn't it thanks to you that I am alive and breathing? But please spare me the rest. The future belongs to those who know how to shape it and, believe me, you won't get anywhere with incantations and animal sacrifices. Only through actions."

I could think of nothing to say. I decided not to discuss the matter further and to take the precautions I thought necessary. However, the issue at stake was so great that I couldn't do without a second opinion. I withdrew to the banks of the River Ormond and called Mama Yaya, Abena, my mother, and Yao. They appeared and I took their relaxed and happy expression to be a reassuring omen.

"You know what they are planning, so what do you advise me to do?"

Yao, who was taciturn, dead or alive, was nevertheless the first to speak.

"It reminds me of a slave revolt when I was young. It had been organized by Ti-Noel, who hadn't yet taken to the mountains and was still sweating it out on the Belleplaine plantation. He had his men stationed everywhere and, at a given signal, they were to burn the Great Houses to ashes."

Something in his voice was warning me and I asked rather abruptly: "Well, how did it end?"

He began to roll a cigar of tobacco leaves, as if he were trying to play for time, then he looked me straight in the eye. "In a bloodbath, as it always does! The time is not ripe for our freedom!"

"When, when will it be?" I asked hoarsely. "How much more blood does there have to be and why?"

The three spirits remained silent, as if I were trying to break the rules again and embarrass them.

"Our memory will have to be covered in blood," Yao continued. "Our memories will have to float to the surface like water lilies."

"Tell me, how much longer?" I insisted.

Mama Yaya shook her head. "There's no end to the misfortunes of black folks."

I was used to her fatalistic words and shrugged my shoulders in irritation. What was the point of arguing?

"Lord of the Air, the Night, and the Waters, You who make the child move in its mother's womb, You who make the sugarcane grow, And fill it with sticky juice. Lord of the Air, the Sun, and the Stars . . ."

I had never prayed so hard. Around me the night was black, shimmering from the smell of blood of the victims piled at my feet.

"Lord of the Present, the Past, and the Future, without whom the earth would not bear fruit, neither coco plum nor jujube nor passion fruit nor *pomme cythère,* nor Congo peas . . ."

I lost myself in prayer.

Shortly before midnight a weak moon curled itself up on a cushion of cloud.

15

Do I have to go on to the end? Hasn't the reader already guessed what is going to happen? So predictable, so easily predictable! And then by telling it, I shall be reliving my suffering over and over again. And must I suffer twice?

Iphigene and his friends left nothing to chance. I don't know how they got the guns. Did they, for example, lay hands on the munitions depot at Oistins or St. James? Our island was full of munitions depots because it had been used in the past as a base for attacking the Spanish possessions and it continued to live in fear of the French. Whatever the case, I began to see guns, powder, and bullets piling up in front of the house; Iphigene and his henchmen doled them out in equal parts. I don't know how they had reckoned up the number of estates in operation (844 in all) and the men they could count on. I could hear them checking off names and figures: "Ti-Roro from Bois Debout: three guns and three pounds of powder. Nevis from Castleridge: twelve guns. Bois Sans Soif from Pumpkitt: seven guns and four pounds of powder."

And scouts went out in all directions, taking cover under the trees and in the tall grass. At one point Iphigene looked so tired that I begged him: "Come and lie down a while. What's the use of dying before you've won?"

He waved his hand impatiently, but nevertheless he obeyed me and came to sit down beside me. I stroked his rough, woolly hair, reddened by the sun.

"I have often talked to you about my life. But there's one thing I haven't told you. I was once pregnant and I had to do away with the baby. It seems to me you have come back in its place."

He shrugged his shoulders. "I sometimes wonder where you women get all your imagination from."

He then got up. "Have you ever thought I don't want you to treat me like a son?"

He went out.

I preferred not to think too much about the meaning of his words. Besides, was there time? The countdown had started: only one more night before the attack. I was not really worried about the outcome of the plot. In fact, I tried not to think about it. I let my mind blur in colored dreams and I concentrated above all on my baby. She had started to move in my womb; a sort of slow, gentle creeping as if she wanted to explore her confined quarters. I imagined her as a blind tadpole with a mop of hair, floating, swimming, trying unsuccessfully to turn on her back and stubbornly starting over and over again. A little longer and we would be looking at each other and her fresh gaze would make me ashamed of my wrinkles and my stumps of teeth. My daughter would settle old scores for me! She would know how to win the love of a man with a heart as warm as corn bread. He would be faithful to her. They would have children they would teach to see beauty in themselves. Children who would grow straight and free toward the sky.

Around five o'clock Iphigene brought me a rabbit he had stolen from someone's hutch. He was holding it by the ears. I usually don't mind killing animals for sacrifices, but I shuddered at the thought of killing these innocent animals men use for food. I have never slit a single chicken's throat or gutted a single fish without asking its forgiveness for the evil I was inflicting on it. In an awkward movement I sat down heavily under the awning I used as a kitchen and began to gut the animal. As I slit open its belly a stream of black, stinking blood spattered my face, while two rotting balls of flesh wrapped in a green membrane rolled onto the ground. I recoiled at the smell and my knife fell from my hands and stuck in my left foot. I let out a scream and Iphigene threw down the gun he was cleaning and came to my rescue.

He drew the knife out of my flesh and tried to stop the blood from gushing forth. It seemed this tiny wound was going to drain me of all my blood. A small puddle had already formed at my feet, reminding me of Yao's words: "Our memory will be covered in blood. Our memories will float to the surface like water lilies."

After having torn into shreds all the clothes he could get hold of, Iphigene managed to stop the hemorrhage and carried me into the cabin bundled up like a baby.

"Now keep still. I'll look after everything. Who says I can't cook?"

The sharp smell of my blood soon began to irritate my nostrils and it was then I remembered Susanna Endicott. That awful shrew! Hadn't I kept her bundled up like this for months, for years, swimming in her own juice, and wasn't she now getting her revenge just as she had promised? Blood for urine? Of us two, who was the more formidable? I wanted to pray, but my mind wouldn't let me. I remained there, staring through the crisscross of poles that held up the roof.

Shortly afterward, Mama Yaya, Abena, my mother, and Yao came to see me. They had been in North Point calling on an obeah man when they had seen what had happened to me. Mama Yaya tapped me on the shoulder. "It's nothing. Soon you'll forget all about it."

Abena, my mother, of course couldn't help sighing and grumbling. "If there's one thing you're not good at, it's choosing your men. Oh well, soon everything will be back to normal."

I looked her squarely in the face. "What do you mean by that?"

But she turned a pirouette. "How many illegitimate children do you intend to collect? Look at the hair on your head, as white as the flock on the silk-cotton tree."

Yao merely kissed me on the forehead and whispered: "We'll see you later. We'll be there as soon as possible."

Then they disappeared.

Around eight o'clock Iphigene brought me a gourd filled with food. He had managed to cook up a pig's tail, some rice, and black-eyed peas. He changed my dressings, showing no alarm at seeing them drip with blood again.

This was the last night before the final act, when doubt, fear, and cowardice fight it out among themselves! What was the point? Was life so bad after all? Why risk losing it, however meager the scraps of happiness? The last night before the final attack! I was trembling, I didn't dare snuff out the candle, and I could see the monstrous shadow of my body flickering on the wall. Iphigene came and huddled up close to me. I held his strong, slim chest tight to me and I could feel his heart beating wildly.

"Are you afraid as well?" I whispered.

He didn't answer but his hand groped in the dark. Then I realized with amazement what he wanted. Perhaps it was fear? Perhaps he wanted to reassure me? To reassure himself? The desire to taste pleasure one last time? Probably all these feelings combined into one burning and compelling emotion. When his young, hot body pressed itself against mine, my first reaction was to recoil. I was ashamed of offering up my old age to his caresses and I almost pushed him away for I had the absurd feeling of committing incest. Then his desire became contagious. I felt a wave well up inside me. It picked up strength and urgency and then broke. It flooded me, it flooded him, it flooded us and took us under several times to the point where we lost our breath and choked and begged to stop. We were frightened and exhausted when it threw us up on a quiet cove planted with almond trees. We drowned ourselves in kisses and he whispered: "If you knew how much it hurts seeing you carry this child that isn't mine, the child of a man I despise. If you only knew the real face of Christopher and the role he plays. But we are not going to talk about him when death is perhaps sharpening its knives."

"Do you think we'll win?"

He shrugged his shoulders. "What does it matter! The important thing is to have tried and to have refused the fatalism of misfortune!"

I sighed and he hugged me up against him.

Blessed is the love that carries man on the waters of oblivion. That makes him forget he is a slave. That rolls back the torment and the fear. Reassured, Iphigene and I plunged back into the healing waters of sleep. We swam against the current, watching

I, Tituba

the needlefish court the crayfish. We dried our hair under the moon. We did not sleep for long, however. I must confess that once the intoxication had worn off, I felt a little ashamed. This boy could have been my son! Did I no longer have any respect for myself? And then why had so many men passed through my bed? Hester was right when she said: "You're too fond of love, Tituba!"

And I wondered whether this was not a blemish in me, a fault that I should have tried to cure myself of.

Outside, the horse of night galloped on. Clippity-clop. Clippity-clop. Close by my side my son and lover was sleeping. I was unable to do the same. All the events of my life came back to me extremely vividly and the faces of all those I had loved and hated crowded around my bed. Oh, I recognized them all! I could put a name to every face. Betsey, Abigail, Anne Putnam, Goodwife Parris, Samuel Parris, John Indian. At the very moment when my body had proved how frivolous it could be, my heart reminded me that it had never belonged to anybody else but John Indian. What had become of him in that cold and gloomy America?

I knew that more and more slave ships were unloading their cargo on its shores and that America was preparing to dominate the world with the sweat of our brows. I knew that the Indians had been wiped off the map and reduced to roaming the land that once was theirs.

What was John Indian doing in that country that was so hard on us? So hard on the weak, on the dreamers, and on those who do not judge men by their wealth.

The horse of night was galloping on. Clippity-clop. Clippity-clop. And all these faces danced in front of my eyes, vivid as only the creatures of the night can be.

Was it Susanna Endicott taking her revenge? And were her powers greater than mine?

Outside the wind had risen. I could hear it hailing mangoes. I could hear it blow through the calabash tree and rap its fruit. I was afraid. I was cold. I wanted to return to my mother's womb. But at that very instant, my daughter moved as if she were calling for my affection. I laid my hand on my belly and, little by little I was filled with a kind of tranquillity, a kind of lucidity, as if I had resigned myself to the final drama I was about to live.

With my senses sharp, I heard the wind die down. A chicken frightened by a mongoose could be heard squawking in the pen. Then silence fell. And I ended up falling asleep.

    *   *   *

Hardly had I closed my eyes than I had a dream.

I was trying to enter a forest, but the trees were in league against me and black creepers hung down, twining themselves around me. I opened my eyes. The room was full of smoke. I was about to cry out: "But I've been through all this before." Then I realized what was happening.

I shook Iphigene, who was sleeping like a child with a radiant smile on his lips. He opened his eyes, misty from the recollection of his pleasure. Very quickly, however, he realized what was happening and jumped to his feet. I followed, hampered by my wound, which wouldn't stop bleeding. We got out. The cabin was surrounded by soldiers aiming their guns at us.

Who had betrayed us?

    *   *   *

The planters decided to set an example, because this had been the second major revolt in three years. They had secured the help of the English troops that had come to defend the island from outside attacks and nothing had been left to chance. The plantations were systematically searched and any suspect slave was stood under a silk-cotton tree. Then he was driven with the others at bayonet point to a large clearing where dozens of gallows had been erected.

A patch over one eye, Errin surveyed the scene of the executions in the company of his fellow planters. He came up to me and sneered: "Well, witch, what they should have done to you in Boston, we're going to do here! And you'll meet up with your sisters who left before you did! And a good Sabbath to all!"

I didn't answer. I was looking at Iphigene. As the leader he had been hit so hard that he could barely stand and would surely have collapsed if one of the overseers was not making his body jerk with constant lashes of the whip. His face was so swollen that he must have been practically blind and was looking to the sun for warmth rather than light. I cried out to him: "Don't be afraid! Above all, don't be afraid! We'll soon be together again!"

He turned to the spot where my voice came from and as he couldn't speak, he motioned to me with his hand.

His body was the first to swing in the air, hanging from a heavy beam. I was the last to be led to the gallows, for I was to be given special treatment. The punishment that I had "escaped" in Salem was now going to be inflicted on me. A man dressed in an impressive black and red coat read out all my crimes, past and present. I had bewitched the inhabitants of a peaceful, God-fearing village. I had called Satan into their hearts and turned them one against the other in fury. I had set fire to the house of an honest merchant who had decided to disregard my crimes, but who had paid for his lack of judgment with the death of his children. At this point in the inquisition I almost screamed out that it was all untrue and nothing but vile and cruel lies. Then I thought otherwise. What was the point? Soon I would reach a kingdom where the light of truth burns bright and unrelenting. Sitting astride the beam of my gallows, Mama Yaya, Abena, my mother, and Yao were waiting to take me by the hand.

I was the last to be taken to the gallows. All around me strange trees were bristling with strange fruit.

Epilogue

Epilogue

And that is the story of my life. Such a bitter, bitter story.

My real story starts where this one leaves off and it has no
end. Christopher was wrong or probably he wanted to hurt
me—there *is* a song about Tituba! I hear it from one end of
the island to the other, from North Point to Silver Sands, from
Bridgetown to Bottom Bay. It runs along the ridge of the hills.
It is poised on the tip of the heliconia. The other day I heard
a boy four or five years old humming it. In delight, I dropped
three ripe mangoes at his feet and he remained rooted to the
spot, staring up at the tree that had given him such a present
out of season. Yesterday it was a woman beating her wash on
the rocks of the river who was humming it. Out of gratitude I
wrapped myself around her neck and there she was young and
beautiful again, admiring her reflection in the water.

I hear it wherever I go.

When I run to someone's deathbed. When I take the trembling spirit of a dead person in my hands. When I let human
beings catch a glimpse of those they thought they had lost
forever.

For now that I have gone over to the invisible world I continue to heal and cure. But primarily I have dedicated myself to
another task, helped by Iphigene, my son and lover, my companion for eternity. I am hardening men's hearts to fight. I am
nourishing them with dreams of liberty. Of victory. I have been
behind every revolt. Every insurrection. Every act of disobedi-
ence.

Since the unsuccessful rebellion of 17** not a month goes by
without a fire breaking out. Without a poisoning striking down
one Great House after another. Errin went back over the sea

after I ordered the spirits of those he had tortured to play the *gwo-ka* drums night after night around his bed. I accompanied him to the brigantine *Faith* and saw him down glass after glass of rum in the vain hope of ridding his sleep of dreams.

Christopher too tosses and turns on his bed and has lost all taste for his women. I refrain from harming him further, for isn't he the father of my unborn daughter?

I have not crossed the sea to persecute Samuel Parris, the judges, and the preachers. I know that others have done it for me. Samuel Parris's son, the object of so much attention and pride, was to die insane. Cotton Mather was to be dishonored and unmasked by a little vixen. All the judges were to lose their pride. And, as Rebecca Nurse said, the time will come for another judgment. And if I'm not included, what does it matter!

I do not belong to the civilization of the Bible and Bigotry. My people will keep my memory in their hearts and have no need for the written word. It's in their heads. In their hearts and in their heads. Since I died without giving birth to a child, the spirits have allowed me to choose a descendant. I took a long time making up my mind. I spied into every cabin. I looked at the washerwomen breast-feeding. I watched the women working in the sugarcane fields as they laid their nursing babies on piles of old clothes, for want of a better place. I made comparisons, I fingered and prodded and finally I found her, the one I needed: Samantha.

I think I chose her because I watched her come into this world.

I was used to looking after Délices, her mother, a black Creole living in Bottom Bay on the Willoughby plantation. As she had already lost two or three children at birth, this time she had me come as quickly as possible. To stave off his anxiety, her man was downing glass after glass of rum on the veranda. The birth took hours and the baby presented herself in the breech position. The mother was losing both her blood and her strength and her poor exhausted soul had but one wish and that was to slip into the other world. The fetus refused to accompany her and fought furiously to enter the universe from which she was separated by only a fragile valve of flesh. In the end she won and I received into my hands a little baby girl with inquisitive eyes and a determined mouth. I watched her grow up and stumble around on her shaky legs, exploring the purgatory of the plantation, finding her delight in the shape of a cloud, the drooping foliage of an ylang-ylang, or the taste of a bitter orange.

As soon as she knew how to speak, she asked: "Why is Zamba so silly? And why does he let Rabbit sit on his back? Why are we slaves and they masters? Why is there only one God? Shouldn't there be one for the slaves and one for the masters?" As the adults' answers did not satisfy her, she made up her own. Although she knew I was dead through the rumor on the island, she showed no surprise when I first appeared in front of her, as if she fully understood that she had been singled out for a special destiny. Now she follows me fervently. I tell her the secrets I'm allowed to share, the hidden power of herbs and the language of animals. I teach her to look for the invisible shapes in the world, the crisscross of communications, and the signs and the symbols. Once her mother and father are asleep, she joins me in the night that I have taught her to love.

A child I didn't give birth to but whom I chose! What motherhood could be nobler!

Iphigene, my son and lover, has not remained idle. He is trying to bring off that rebellion he was unable to achieve while he was alive. He has chosen himself a son. A little quick-footed Congo boy whom the overseers have already got their eye on. The other day he even started to sing Tituba's song.

I am never alone. There's Mama Yaya, Abena, my mother, Yao, Iphigene, and Samantha.

And then there is my island. We have become one and the same. There isn't one of its footpaths I haven't trod. There isn't one of its streams I haven't bathed in. There isn't one of its silk-cotton trees in whose branches I haven't sat. This constant and extraordinary symbiosis is my revenge for my long solitude in the deserts of America. A vast, cruel land where the spirits only beget evil! Soon they will be covering their faces with hoods, the better to torture us. They will lock up our children behind the heavy gates of the ghettos. They will deny us our rights and blood will beget blood.

I have only one regret, for we invisibles too have our regrets so that we can better relish our share of happiness: it's having to be separated from Hester. We do communicate, of course. I can smell the dried almonds on her breath. I can hear the echo of her laugh. But each of us remains on her side of the ocean. I know that she is pursuing her dreams of creating a world of women that will be more just and humane. I myself have loved men too much and shall continue to do so. Sometimes I get the urge to slip into someone's bed to satisfy a bit of leftover desire and my fleeting lover is delighted with his solitary pleasure.

Yes, I'm happy now. I can understand the past, read the present, and look into the future. Now I know why there is so much suffering and why the eyes of our people are brimming with water and salt. But I know, too, that there will be an end to all this. When? Who knows? I'm in no hurry now that I am free of that impatience that is peculiar to mortals. What is one life in relation to the immensity of time?

Last week a young *bossale* girl committed suicide. She was an Ashanti like my mother. The priest had christened her Laetitia and she jumped on hearing this barbarious and incongruous name. Three times she tried to swallow her tongue. Three times they brought her back to life. I followed her every step and whispered dreams into her ear. Alas! In the morning these dreams left her more desperate than ever. While I was not looking, she managed to snatch a handful of cassava leaves, which she swallowed with some poisonous roots, and the slaves found her stiff, with foam on her lips and the terrible smell of decomposition hanging over her. Such cases remain few and far between and it is more usual for me to keep a slave from the edge of despair by whispering: "Look at the splendor of our island. Soon it will all be ours. Fields of nettles and sugarcane. Furrows of yams and patches of cassava. All of it!"

Sometimes, oddly enough, I feel like changing into mortal form. So I become an *anoli* and draw my knife when the children try to catch me with their straw lassos. Sometimes I become a fighting cock in the pit and the clamor of the crowd sends my head spinning more than the rum. Oh how I love to give the slave the excitement of winning! Off he goes, dancing and brandishing his fist, a gesture that will soon symbolize other victories. Sometimes I become a bird and tease the slingshots of the young scamps when they shout: "Got it!" I fly off with a rustle of wings and laugh at their faces. Sometimes I become a goat and caper around Samantha, who is no fool. For this child of mine has learned to recognize my presence in the twitching of an animal's coat, the crackling of a fire between four stones, the rainbow-hued babbling of the river, and the sound of the wind as it whistles through the great trees on the hills.

Historical Note

Glossary

Afterword

Bibliography

Historical Note

The witch trials of Salem began in March 1692 with the arrests of Sarah Good, Sarah Osborne, and Tituba, who confessed her "crime." Sarah Osborne died in prison in May 1692. Nineteen women were hanged and one man, Giles Corey, was sentenced to a *peine forte et dure* (pressed to death). On 21 February 1693, Sir William Phips, governor of the Bay Colony, sent a report to London on the subject of witchcraft. He submitted the cases of over fifty women who still remained in prison and requested permission to relieve their suffering. This was accorded in May 1693, when the last of the accused were granted a general pardon and released. The Reverend Samuel Parris left the village of Salem in 1697, after a long quarrel with its inhabitants concerning arrears in salary and firewood. His wife had died the previous year giving birth to a son, Noyes.

Around 1693 Tituba, our heroine, was sold for the price of her prison fees and the cost of her chains and shackles. To whom? Such is the intentional or unintentional racism of the historians that we shall never know. According to Anne Petry, a black American novelist who also became passionately interested in our heroine, Tituba was bought by a weaver and spent the rest of her days in Boston.

A vague tradition says Tituba was sold to a slave dealer, who took her back to Barbados.

I myself have given her an ending of my own choosing.

The reader should note that the village of Salem is now called Danvers. It is the town of Salem—where most of the trials, but not the mass hysteria, took place—that has become famous for its history of witchcraft.

MARYSE CONDÉ

Glossary

acoma: (*Sideroxylon mastichodendron*), commonly known in the anglophone West Indies as mastic bully.

ajoupa: a word of Carib origin designating a small thatched hut.

akwaba: Ashanti greeting meaning "welcome."

anoli: a small lizard of the family Iguanidae.

azalée-des-azalées: a literary invention by the author.

bossale: Guineaman or Guineawoman, a slave just unloaded from Africa.

calenda: of unknown origin; here used in an old slave song.

crick, crack!: The traditional opening to a story told by a West Indian storyteller in front of an audience.

grangreks: scholars; Creole for "grands Grecs."

gwo-ka: ka means drum in Creole; *gwo-ka* is a popular drumbeat in the French West Indies.

kippa: Hebrew word for the skullcap worn by Jews.

konoko: slave's white canvas trousers.

Minnah: afternoon prayers in the Jewish faith.

mougué: word of unknown African origin in the Creole slave song sung by John Indian.

passiflorinde: a literary invention by the author.

persulfureuse: a literary invention by the author.

pomme-cythère: (*Spondias dulcis*) a delicious fruit used in drinks and preserves. It is not poisonous, as the author suggests.

Populara indica: a literary invention by the author.

prune taureau: a literary invention by the author.

rayo: (*Cordyline terminalis*) a shrub commonly used for hedges marking boundaries in the West Indies.

Glossary

salapertuis: a literary invention by the author.

sheep without horns: a man.

soukougnan: literally, "bloodsucker"; word derived from the African language of the Tukulör people, where it designates a spirit that attacks humans and drinks their blood like a vampire.

Afterword

The Guadeloupean novelist Maryse Condé's *Moi, Tituba, sorcière . . . noire de Salem* (I, Tituba, black witch of Salem) was, in 1986, the first francophone Caribbean novel to connect the English Caribbean with the colonial United States, and the first of Condé's already numerous works to successfully combine an introspective journey with an examination of what it means to be Caribbean. *Tituba* invited fresh consideration of the question of identity in the Caribbean context, and it marked an important step on the path to self-discovery for the author. Furthermore, Condé's creation of a mock-epic protagonist and her use of postmodern irony in her novel opened up a new literary space for writers from the region, truly blowing apart the status quo. Because the historical Tituba was actually Barbadian, Condé uses Barbados instead of Guadeloupe as the Caribbean locale, but she infers similar circumstances from the history of slavery and domination common to the region.

Writing by authors from the French overseas departments of Guadeloupe, Martinique, and French Guiana has focused on the question of identity since the 1940s. This seems only natural. French colonialism began in the Caribbean in 1635 and was "perfected" by the systematization of slavery as an economic institution in the *Code noir* (Slave laws), written by Louis XIV's controller general of finance Jean-Baptiste Colbert and promulgated in 1685. The ensuing colonial order imposed an experience of double alienation on the people of color of the region, forcing them into a historical void and a partial cultural vacuum. In the first place, the only recorders of local history were French colonists, who told the story from their point of view. Furthermore, the black slaves who were brought to the Americas were systematically separated from their fel-

188

Afterword

low tribesmen, so that the cultures they might have brought with them survived only in fragments. The culture they developed in the New World was born of encounters with people from other parts of Africa and of interaction with the Indians who were already on the islands in the Caribbean Sea. Ignored for the most part by the French colonists, today the heritage of the Arawak and Carib Indians of Martinique and Guadeloupe is celebrated in the departmental museums in Fort-de-France and Le Moule, respectively.

French and English Caribbean plantation societies, like their American counterpart, engendered personal humiliation, individual isolation, and obedience to the Other who claimed total power. Thus, the absence of nonwhite Caribbean historians was exacerbated by a devaluation of the self, which intensified the need for an eventual focus on identity. Under slavery and the political and economic bondage that followed, interdependence within the group (the individual's only means of survival) had to be nurtured but carefully hidden. The plantation space privileged women and feminine sensitivity, because black women had the work of creating the hearth and holding their society together. Teaching the children and transmitting the culture that evolved on the plantation, these women also often dominated the white master's entire household: his bedroom, his nursery, and his kitchen. Women thus became the mainstay of Caribbean culture; this tradition is one reason why there are so many women writers in the area today.

The only nonwhite heroes and heroines in the Caribbean were the maroons, fugitive slaves who lived in the hills outside the confines of established plantation society and caused as much damage as they could, through mass poisonings, mass murders, and the burning of plantations. Although Edouard Glissant points out in *Le discours antillais* (1981; *Caribbean Discourse*, CARAF Books edition, 1989) that these runaway slaves have not generally served as models of revolt and hope in the past, today they do so in Caribbean literature, where their motif appears constantly in one form or another. *Tituba* is in some respects an exception because of the postmodern irony with which the subject is treated.

Afterword

After the abolition of slavery in 1848, blacks in the French overseas colonies were entitled by law to education, but the transition from illiterate slave to literate freeman was painfully slow, just as it was in the United States after the Civil War. Even when Guadeloupe, Martinique, and French Guiana became overseas departments of France in 1946, they continued to suffer from domination by the ex-colonial capital, which French speakers call *le métropole* (the metropolis). Today a third of the French Caribbean people live in continental France, where they have migrated in search of jobs or higher education. In addition to the problem of migration, there is the reality that the overseas departments depend upon the mother country for many supplies and staples, including food items. One university has been created for the entire region, the Université Antilles-Guyane. The projected removal of trade and employment restrictions among the countries of the European Common Market in 1993 poses potential problems for the autonomy and livelihood of citizens of the French Caribbean. Individuals from countries outside France who cannot now work in the French Caribbean because they are not French citizens may then be attracted to settle in the islands, thus further exacerbating the existing unemployment problem.

It is symptomatic of their postcolonial malaise that the French themselves have not shown much interest in French Caribbean literature to date. Maryse Condé has fared better than most writers: ˋ*Ségou, les murailles de terre* (Segou: The walls of earth) was a best-seller and was a selection by Le livre du mois (book-of-the-month club) in 1984, the year of its publication; *Moi, Tituba, sorcière . . . noire de Salem* won the Grand prix littéraire de la femme in 1986. A few other writers in addition to Condé have been taken up by the big French publishers, Edouard Glissant and Daniel Maximin by Le Seuil, Raphaël Confiant and Xavier Orville by Bernard Grasset, and Patrick Chamoiseau by Gallimard. However, most writers have to go to smaller, specialized houses like Présence africaine, Editions caribéennes, and L'Harmattan to get into print. In addition, the French press except for *La quinzaine littéraire*—a bimonthly literary magazine—appears to be almost unaware that these writers exist. Indeed, it seems that most francophone Caribbean writers will have to become known abroad in translation before they become known in France.

The initial literary impetus for contemporary francophone Caribbean literature was the negritude movement. Conceived in Paris in the 1930s by three university students from different parts of the African diaspora, Aimé Césaire of Martinique, Léon-Gontran Damas of French Guiana, and Léopold Sédar Senghor of Senegal, negritude promoted the validation of the black person's ethnic identity and asserted the right to self-expression. There was no negritude movement as such, however, before the Second World War, which brought to the surface the racial antagonisms that characterized the social structure of the French West Indies.

The revalorization of black West Indians' identity began during the war on the neighboring island of Martinique. In 1941, Aimé Césaire and his wife, Suzanne, founded *Tropiques* (Tropics), a magazine of Martinican culture, along with their friend and fellow lycée teacher the Marxist writer René Ménil. Read primarily by students, *Tropiques* became more and more political and was banned by local representatives of the Vichy government in 1943 for its subversive intent. The reprinting of *Tropiques* in 1978 immediately preceded a renewed interest in the Caribbean region outside France in the 1980s. In the interview he gave for the reissue of *Tropiques*, Aimé Césaire emphasizes the importance of the individual writer's personal inspiration and affirms the fact that his own writing was originally born of a passionate intolerance for the collective condition of the Martinican people.

Caribbean cultures in particular needed to reaffirm the values that had permitted slaves and their descendants to survive, because creativity had been stifled in one way or another by slavery and its aftermath, as Maryse Condé pointed out in her essay *La civilisation du bossale* (The culture of the bush nigger, 1978), in which she discusses the oral literature of Guadeloupe and Martinique. Condé demonstrates that the nature of the slaves' dependence on the master engendered hostility and aggressiveness as well as a thirst for justice that could not be quenched. She argues that creativity could not flourish in those harsh conditions. Showing how Caribbean folktales became a way of redefining the slaves' universe, she concludes her essay by suggesting that another kind of literature, an epic, historic literature, with other values was needed. This new literature is precisely the kind she and others are writing today.

The true cornerstone of French Caribbean literature is Aimé Césaire's long poem *Cahier d'un retour au pays natal* (Notebook of a return to the native land). The *Cahier*, which has been republished at least nine times, including four translations into English and two into Spanish, recounts the poverty of daily life in Martinique, laments the enormous losses suffered by Caribbean people, explores the poet's own anguish, and then celebrates the internal power of Caribbean space in a final self-revelatory movement culminating in a call to action.[1]

The negritude movement, by identifying itself exclusively with Afro-Caribbean ethnicity, failed to account for the true diversity of this multicultural region. It fell to Edouard Glissant, Martinican novelist, poet, critic, and theoretician of *Le discours antillais*, to transcend these limitations. Glissant coined the neologism *Antillanité* or Caribbeanness, which he defines as the documentation and celebration of the hybrid cultural heritage of the Caribbean region. He explains that contemporary writers must fill in the voids left by past historiography and bring the traditions of the collectivity to surface expression after centuries of silence: "The rupture of the slave trade, then the experience of slavery, introduces between blind belief and clear consciousness a gap that we have never finished filling. The absence of representation, of echo, of any sign, makes this emptiness forever yawn under our feet. Along with our real-

1. Although a preoriginal version of *Cahier d'un retour au pays natal* was published in the magazine *Volontés* in Paris in 1939, the poem's public life began with Brentano's New York edition in 1947, as A. James Arnold points out in his Introduction to the CARAF Books edition of Césaire's *Lyric and Dramatic Poetry, 1946–82* (Charlottesville: University Press of Virginia, 1990), p. xi. Readers may wish to consult the translation of *Notebook of a Return to the Native Land* by Clayton Eshleman and Annette Smith (Berkeley: University of California Press, 1983).

Afterword

ization of the process of exploitation (along with any action we take), we must articulate the unexpressed while moving beyond it: expressions of 'popular belief' are a nonpossession that we must confirm; to the point where, recognizing them as a nonpossession, we will really deal with them by abandoning them."[2]

Glissant calls for an exploded literary discourse, posing the problem of inventing new forms of expression and articulating the necessity of confronting and mastering the Caribbean obsession with the fractured past. His fifth novel, *Mahogany* (1987), with its multivalent, fragmented structure and internal forms of *marronnage* (marooning), is as profound an attempt to participate in the creation of a new antipoetics as are Daniel Maximin's *L'Isolé soleil* (1981; *Lone Sun*, CARAF Books edition, 1989) and Maryse Condé's *I, Tituba, Black Witch of Salem.*

After negritude and Caribbeanness, "creoleness" is the third and most recent attempt to express the current state of francophone Caribbean literature and culture. This term emerged in 1989 with the publication of *Eloge de la créolité* (In praise of creoleness) by Jean Bernabé, Patrick Chamoiseau, and Raphaël Confiant. Not to be confused with the creole language, creoleness privileges the exploration of the self, urging the writer to go beyond the process of recuperating the past. However, it also reaffirms Césaire's search for internal inspiration and Glissant's validation of multiple origins and the search for lost history. Bernabé, Chamoiseau, and Confiant explain that they favor the celebration of the diverse fabric of Caribbean society along with a liberated, nonauthoritarian expression of that diversity. Hence, the creoleness of 1989 can be interpreted as a re-visioning of Césaire's negritude of the 1940s and Glissant's Caribbeanness of the 1980s.

During my May 1991 interview with Maryse Condé for this CARAF Books edition of *Tituba* (see below), she indicated her belief that creoleness must be transcended, emphasizing that the writer must explore more than his/her own island world.

2. Edouard Glissant, *Caribbean Discourse: Selected Essays,* trans. J. Michael Dash (Charlottesville: University Press of Virginia, 1989), 201.

Afterword

Like Maximin's *L'Isolé soleil, I Tituba, Black Witch of Salem* expresses and gives a formal and historical content to the ideal of creoleness, in that it celebrates Tituba's unique voice and resists being locked into existing categories of francophone Caribbean literature. Most re-visionings of French Caribbean history have primarily attempted to recuperate the lost past. Condé, however, *uses* the lost past to dominate the present and open the future to new directions. In this novel she mounts a resounding attack on the hypocrisy that characterized Puritan New England; she invites an examination of the entire system of slavery; she implies criticism of racism and religious bigotry in contemporary America; she castigates men's domination of women; and she parodies modern feminist discourse.

The European novel is another integral part of the heritage of French Caribbean literature, because the school system as it existed in France was transported in its entirety to the colonies: teachers, texts, and materials. The French tried to create among their colonial subjects an elite that was as well educated as its French counterpart, and Maryse Condé's bourgeois family offers a good example of the result. French *is* the language in which most French Caribbean writers work most comfortably, Maryse Condé among them. Nevertheless, even though they also speak Creole more or less fluently, francophone Caribbean writers have always used the European tradition to give voice to an expression of their own experience. Just as Aimé Césaire used surrealism to inscribe his personal psychic reality in postwar versions of his *Cahier d'un retour au pays natal* and as Joseph Zobel used the form of the social realist novel in 1950 in *La rue cases-nègres* (Black shack alley), so today Maryse Condé in *Traversée de la mangrove* (Journey through the mangrove, 1988), Edouard Glissant in *Mahogany,* and Daniel Maximin in *L'Isolé soleil* and *Soufrières* (The Soufrière; brothers and sisters, 1989) use postmodern narrative strategies of fragmented and self-reflexive discourse, multiple narrators, and nonlinear chronology to express their visions of the present.

Sounding the theme of artistic independence she had addressed in *La parole des femmes* (Women's voice, 1979), Condé explained the current situation in our May 1991 interview. She stressed the point that francophone Caribbean writers need to

Afterword

be considered first and foremost as writers—not as "French Caribbean" writers—by themselves and by the broader reading public. They must be free to follow their own vision of reality and to express the bulk of the experience that they have gained in the world, rather than limiting themselves to a depiction of life in the "French" Caribbean.

Condé's distaste for labels of any kind results in part from her childhood experience of having been taught to accept a very restricted vision of her native country. As the daughter of successful, upwardly mobile bourgeois parents, she was supposed to be proud of being a person of color but to look down on everything from the West Indies, including the Creole language. An avid reader who secretly borrowed books from her father's extensive library, Maryse had read most of the great French novels before she was twelve, but it was not until she was a lycée student in Paris that she learned of her own Caribbean literary heritage. She is fond of telling the story that it was a white classmate, the daughter of liberal French parents, who first introduced her to Césaire's *Cahier d'un retour au pays natal*.

Condé chose to become reacquainted with her island on her own terms only after she had lived in Paris and then in Africa for a number of years. Her celebration of the British West Indies in *I, Tituba, Black Witch of Salem* is on the one hand a gesture of affection for the Caribbean and on the other a prelude to her return home in 1986. Today she speaks of having learned to understand Guadeloupe, and she has said how essential it was for her to return to the island and get to know people from all segments of that diverse society. In an interview with Vèvè Clark, Condé tells of this homecoming: "I went out and met with not so much the people but the island itself. I learned how the island speaks to your mind; how it smells. It has a life of its own despite the meanness of individuals or their limitations. So, yes, I made peace with the island and having done so, I also made peace with myself in a way."[3]

3. Vèvè Clark, "I Have Made Peace with My Island: An Interview with Maryse Condé," *Callaloo* 12, no. 1 (1989): 133.

Afterword

Although Maryse Condé tells us that Tituba's personal story has no relationship to her own life experience, the fabric of both journeys is woven of the same cloth. Tituba and Condé both attack life directly, courageously, and imaginatively. The force of moral honesty sustains them in their quests for real relationships in a world where class differences and racism impede human communication.

In 1959, when she was twenty-two years old, Maryse married Mamadou Condé despite her family's strong objection to him on the grounds that he was "an actor; he had no money, no education."[4] Glad to leave the closed circle of West Indians in Paris, Condé moved to her husband's native Guinea, where she soon realized that the marriage was a mistake. Leaving her husband, she went alone to the Ivory Coast, where she taught school and gave birth to their first daughter. She moved back to Guinea, had two more daughters, and then left her husband for good in 1964. Condé's willingness to defy her family in her marriage, breaking class and racial barriers they tried to impose, and her courage in admitting subsequently that her marriage was not good, demonstrate how directly she approaches life's challenges.

Finding original ways of looking at literature in her critical works and daring to address fresh topics in her novels, Condé's body of work shows the same kind of courage and determination as her personal life. Her willingness to write about what is on her mind without camouflaging her intent manifested itself in her first novel, *Hérémakhonon*, published in 1976. There she wrote of Veronica, a young West Indian woman who goes to Paris and then to Africa in search of herself. Full of negative memories of her childhood in Guadeloupe, Veronica discovers that Africa does not satisfy her either. Drawn to the political left, she also has an affair with the dictator who controls the country. She flees the country at the end of the novel, tormented and angered by the unnecessary bloodshed, alone and uncertain still. Characterized by irony and ambiguity, *Héré-*

4. Ibid., p. 99.

makhonon "represented the first time that someone denounced
Sékou Touré and African Socialism in writing."[5]

Condé's second novel, *Une saison à Rihata* (A season in
Rihata, 1981), takes place in an unnamed African country and
focuses on individual morality and political corruption. Condé
explores adultery and human psychology by examining the
stagnant marriage of Marie-Hélène, a middle-aged and disillu-
sioned woman from the French Caribbean, and her African
husband, Zek. Condé's narrative style shows that life is much
more complex than we think, by weaving the separate plot lines
together in such a way that the reader cannot understand the
full story until the last pages of the text.

Greatly acclaimed in France, alternately praised and denounced by African scholars, Condé's third novel appeared
in two volumes: *Ségou: Les murailles de terre* and *Ségou: La
terre en miettes* (Segou: The earth in pieces, 1985). Contro-
versy about the novel centered on what was real, what was
fiction, and whether Condé claimed anthropological expertise
in her depiction. At all events, *Ségou* is a lively narrative that
recounts through brief introspective passages the detailed saga
of religious and social history in Africa and the Caribbean,
highlighting the encounter between Islam and African animism
and plantation slave society in Brazil.

Following the publication of her fourth novel, *I, Tituba*, in
1986, Condé's fifth and sixth novels focus on the francophone
Caribbean. *La vie scélérate* (Wicked life, 1987) depicts the
social history of three generations of a Guadeloupean family.
This linear narrative, enhanced by interior monologues and
flashbacks, offers Condé's fullest portrait to date of the ambi-
ance in which she grew up and provides an illuminating picture
of the relationship between the French Caribbean islands and
Paris. *Traversée de la mangrove* (Journey through the mangrove, 1989), a Faulknerian text with multiple narrators, paints
a vivid picture of life in a small Caribbean village, as numerous
inhabitants reveal their personal connections with a stranger
who has just died. Speaking about writing *Traversée de la man-*

5. Ibid., p. 121.

grove, Condé says: "Writing is like going on a journey to find something one dreams of. It is like crossing a mangrove with its entangled roots, its pools of briny water and its many layers of mud to reach the sea. It is like mapping a dark and rebellious land."[6]

Condé's most recent novel, *Les derniers rois mages* (The last magi), was published in the spring of 1992. In addition to her novels, Condé has published a collection of two francophone Caribbean folktales under the title *Pays-mêlé* (Land of mixed blood, 1985), and she has written six plays: "Le morne de Massabielle" (The hills of Massabielle, 1972), *Dieu nous l'a donné* (God gave it to us, 1972), *La mort d'Oluwémi d'Ajumako* (The death of Oluwémi d'Ajumako, 1973), "Les sept voyages de Ti-Noel" (Ti-Noel's seven journeys, 1986), *Pension les alizés* (Trade winds guesthouse, 1988), and "Comédie d'amour" (Comedy of love, 1989). The folktales explore magic, love, social class, and family relationships in a Caribbean village, suggesting that the human heart cannot be found guilty for what it feels. The plays, some written specifically for local theater groups in Guadeloupe, concern exile in the lives of people from the islands and a love affair between a Haitian political refugee and an elderly actress, among other subjects.

Condé believes that contemporary French Caribbean writers should become involved with groups of local artists in order to bring their work to the people. She herself is associated with Plus Bakanal, a group that performed "Les sept voyages de Ti Noël" to an audience of two thousand on 27 May 1987, the anniversary date of the abolition of slavery in Guadeloupe in 1848.

Condé's critical work is almost as extensive as her fiction. Besides the studies already mentioned above, she has published *La poésie antillaise* (West Indian poetry, 1977), *Le roman antillais* (the West Indian novel, 1977), and an essay on Césaire's *Cahier d'un retour au pays natal.* She is currently editing two more works, a collection of excerpts from Caribbean literature translated by Richard Philcox and *L'héritage de Caliban* (Cali-

6. Maryse Condé in a letter to the author dated 14 July 1991.

ban's inheritance), a group of critical essays on West Indian literature by prominent scholars.

One of the most politically active writers of the present day, Condé is a longtime supporter of independence from France for Guadeloupe, Martinique, and French Guiana. A member of UPLG, Union pour la libération de la Guadeloupe (Coalition for Guadeloupe's freedom), she was a candidate for the regional council in the March 1992 elections. Generous with her time, Condé has given numerous personal interviews and public lectures, she has contributed pieces to collections honoring other writers, and she remains active in her career as a professor of literature, teaching regularly in universities in the United States.

If one reads all of Condé's novels together, one observes an evolution in setting, form, and content. Starting in Africa with her first three novels, *Hérémakhonon, Une saison à Rihata,* and *Ségou,* Condé moved to the United States and the British West Indies in *I, Tituba, Black Witch of Salem* and then to the francophone Caribbean, specifically Guadeloupe, in *La vie scélérate* and *Traversée de la mangrove.* This geographical movement parallels Condé's emotional journey home to Guadeloupe, and the stylistic changes reveal an ever-deepening concern with artistic form.

The notion of the writer as maroon is central to the Caribbean literary tradition, born of a society where the maroon's initiative, courage, and passion for liberty kept a small part of the people's heritage alive. Condé has already shown herself to be a most productive maroon, and her fourth novel, *I, Tituba, Black Witch of Salem* certainly reveals her capacity to both promote independence for others and claim it for herself. We explored the genesis of this novel, among other topics, in our recent interview.

An Interview with Maryse Condé

A S : *How did you first learn about Tituba?*

M C : *Toward the end of 1985, while in Paris, I was approached by Mme. Gallimard of the Mercure de*

France publishing house to write the story of a female heroine of my region, the Caribbean. I thought of writing about Suzanne Césaire or about the Cuban singer Celia Cruz. Then I rejected the idea, as I was already working on La vie scélérate. *However, it was still in the back of my mind. A few months later, I was a Fulbright scholar in residence at Occidental College in Los Angeles, and I went to the UCLA Library in search of documentation. I got lost in the huge building and found myself in the history section in front of a shelf full of books about the Salem witch trials. Looking through them, I discovered the existence of Tituba, whom I had never heard of before. This story may seem farfetched. However, it is entirely true.*

A S: *Did you feel that you were destined to write about her?*

M C: *I just felt interested by the story and curious to see what happened to Tituba. It is only when I started asking people and historians around me, and did not discover anything factual about her, that I decided I was going to write her story out of my own dreams. I felt that this eclipse of Tituba's life was completely unjust. I felt a strong solidarity with her, and I wanted to offer her her revenge by inventing a life such as she might perhaps have wished it to be told. I began with what was actually known—marriage in Barbados to John Indian, then the departure for Salem in the American colonies, where she took care of the children of her master, the minister Samuel Parris.*

A S: *Have similar coincidences inspired you to write any of your other novels?*

M C: *In the case of* Tituba *it is a bit dramatic. But whatever the novel that you write and the stories that you tell, you have to start with a kind of shock and you feel that you are compelled to write about a certain topic. Tituba was a person, she came to me in that form. But whatever I write, I always have the feeling that something stronger than myself forces me, urges me, to go on writing.*

A S: *You have told me that Tituba helped write her own book, in a sense. Did you begin your conversations with her right away?*

M C: *The conversations went on all the time I was writing the novel. I had the feeling that Tituba was involved in the writing. Even when I left my pages at night in my study, I believed that she would go look at them, read them, and eventually correct what she did not like. I cannot say when we really started conversing, however. All along during my writing of the novel I felt that she was there—that I was addressing her.*

A S: *What is your reaction to Ann Petry's novel about Tituba?*

M C: *I read her novel when I was already halfway through* Tituba *because her book was difficult to find . . . it seems to me it was out of print, or something like that. I was a bit surprised and at the same time slightly disappointed because Ann Petry turned the story into a book for adolescents. For her the story of Tituba was a story of courage in the face of adversity. It was a lesson of hope and dynamism. This was not the type of story that I wanted to tell. For me the interest lies in Tituba's own destiny. So, Ann Petry's story and mine are written from very different viewpoints. I like hers, of course, but I am not interested in giving models to young people.*

A S: *Have you spoken to Ann Petry about your common interest?*

M C: *No, never.*

A S: *Did you feel you were writing a historical novel?*

M C: *For me* Tituba *is not a historical novel.* Tituba *is just*

*the opposite of a historical novel. I was not interested
at all in what her real life could have been. I had few
precise documents: her deposition testimony. It forms
the only historical part of the novel, and I was not
interested in getting anything more than that. I really
invented Tituba. I gave her a childhood, an adolescence, an old age. At the same time I wanted to turn
Tituba into a sort of female hero, an epic heroine, like
the legendary "Nanny of the maroons." I hesitated
between irony and a desire to be serious. The result
is that she is a sort of mock-epic character. When she
was leading the fight of the maroons, it was a parody
somehow.*

A S: *How would you describe the difference between a
historian and a writer?*

M C: *A historian is somebody who studies the facts, the
historical facts—somebody who is tied to reality,
somebody who is tied to what actually happens. I
am just a dreamer—my dreams rest upon a historical basis. Being a black person, having a certain past,
having a certain history behind me, I want to explore
that realm and of course I do it with my imagination
and with my intuition. But I am not involved in any
kind of scholarly research.*

A S: *How did you find out about Puritan New England?*

M C: *There was a historian teaching at the same college,
and I asked her to give me some information about
the Puritans of New England. Because she was Jewish, she influenced me to show how petty the Puritans
really were, how their minds were narrow, full of
prejudice. The Puritans were opposed not only to
the blacks, but also to the Jews. They forbade the
Jews to settle in the colony of Massachusetts, and
forced them to go to the more liberal colony of Rhode
Island. Because of this colleague of mine, the character of the Jew that you see in Tituba came into reality.*

It is because of her that I decided to give Tituba a Jewish lover and that I tried to associate discrimination against the Jews with discrimination against the blacks. It seems to me that it is important that I met her at that time. Of course, she did not know what I was writing about. She did not alter directly what I was trying to do. But she changed my mind in a way.

A S: *Some of your American readers will be familiar with Arthur Miller's play* The Crucible. *Did you use that piece as a source of information?*

M C: *I saw an adaptation of the play in Paris while I was a student. It did not impress me. While I was working on my novel, I did not take the trouble to reread* The Crucible. *I knew that Miller as a white male writer would not pay attention to a black woman.*

A S: *Tell me about Hester Prynne. Do you incorporate her in the novel to subvert further both the male and the American versions of history, as suggested by Clarisse Zimra, or are there other reasons?*[7]

M C: *First of all, I like the novel* The Scarlet Letter *and I read it often. Second, it is set in roughly the same period as* Tituba. *Third, when I went to Salem to visit the village, the place where Tituba used to live, I saw the house of Nathaniel Hawthorne, the House of the Seven Gables . . . meaning there was a link between Tituba and Nathaniel Hawthorne. I didn't know whether I wanted to subvert existing versions of history because all those kinds of reflections are observations from a critical point of view. When you are involved in your writing, you do not have that distance between yourself and your text and you cannot answer this way.*

7. Clarisse Zimra, "His/tory in the Text: Maryse Condé's Tituba," Unpublished paper presented at the African Studies Association annual meeting, October 1989.

Afterword

A S : Would it be accurate to say that your focus was on
Tituba, and you explored the Puritans in order to
imagine her reality?

M C : Writing Tituba was an opportunity to express my feelings about present-day America. I wanted to imply
that in terms of narrow-mindedness, hypocrisy, and
racism, little has changed since the days of the Puritans.

A S : That is a very strong statement! Would you please
elaborate?

M C : Every black person living in America will tell you that
racism still exists. A few success stories that are told
over and over again for propaganda reasons must not
hide the fact that for the majority of the blacks, life
is still hell. As a foreigner and a French-speaking person, I don't suffer directly from it. On the contrary,
I am a curiosity; but I am too lucid not to see how
the society works. Being in contact with many young
black people as a university professor, I can see how
frustrated and frightened they are by their society and
how they have little hope in the future.

A S : You showed us your ability to use history in Ségou:
Les murailles de terre and Ségou: La terre en miettes.
I am wondering now if you actively choose to entice
the reader by creating historical verisimilitude?

M C : As I said, for a black person, history is a challenge
because a black person is supposed not to have any
history except the colonial one. We hardly know what
happened to our people before the time when they met
the Europeans who decided to give them what they
call civilization. For a black person from the West
Indies or from Africa, whatever, for somebody from
the diaspora, I repeat it is a kind of challenge to find
out exactly what was there before. It is not history
for the sake of history. It is searching for one's self,

searching for one's identity, searching for one's origin in order to better understand oneself.

A S : *I would argue that* Tituba *exemplifies Glissant's notion of Caribbeanness in that it fills in blank spaces from lost history, giving voice to the silenced collectivity. How would that strike you?*

M C : *I won't use such generalities. I was attracted to write the particular story of* Tituba *because this woman was unjustly treated by history. I felt the need to give her a reality that was denied to her because of her color and her gender.*

A S : *Is there a connection between Tituba's humanity and her being Caribbean?*

M C : *I shall parody Aimé Césaire and say that "No race has the monopoly on anything." I believe that there is humanity everywhere and not only in the Caribbean.*

A S : *Were you already thinking of writing about Caribbean space when you discovered Tituba as a subject?*

M C : *You could say yes, because when I wrote* Tituba, *I had just decided to come back to Guadeloupe. After* Ségou: Les murailles de terre *and* Ségou: La terre en miettes, *I had decided never to write about Africa again because the book was so terribly received by Africans and Africanists. They took the opportunity to write so much nonsense about the West Indians and their so-called intuition of Africa that I was hurt. Tituba came to me or I came to her (as you prefer) at a period of my life when really I wanted to turn toward the Caribbean and start writing about the Caribbean.*

A S : *Could you have written* Tituba *when you first began writing, say when you wrote* Hérémakhonon? *Why or why not?*

M C : *It would have been impossible. At the time when I*

Afterword

wrote Hérémakhonon, *I was living in West Africa and very much concerned with the problems of that continent. I did not know America. I had never traveled there and knew nothing about its history.*

A S: *Concerning* Hérémakhonon, *what circumstances led to the reissue of this novel as* En attendant le bonheur *(Waiting for happiness)?*

M C: *The novel was badly received. The Guadeloupeans and the Martinicans did not like the picture of their society. The Africans objected to the image of Africa. The Marxists did not like the denunciation of the evils of so-called African Socialism. The militants objected to Veronica, the central character, as a negative heroine, and the feminists hated her because she looked for her liberation through men. What else? However, it is now proven that this novel possesses a sort of lasting appeal. Fifteen years after its publication, there is no colloquium or meeting or conference in this field without one or two papers on* Hérémakhonon. *This means that although people challenge or criticize or even denigrate that novel, they cannot overlook it. For these reasons, the publisher, who was very fond of it and believed that it probably was my best novel, decided to reissue it in a more attractive format (with a new cover, a new title, and a preface to explain the circumstances of its genesis). There was also a strong demand from the readers who could not find it in bookstores.*

A S: *Did you originally plan a more hermetic title for* Tituba *as you did with* Une saison à Rihata *and* Hérémakhonon?

M C: *I wanted to call it simply* I, Tituba *but the publishers said that was a bit laconic as a title and added* Black Witch of Salem.

A S: *What part of your own background relates to* Tituba?

Afterword

M C: *No part at all.*

A S: *Tell me about your knowledge of witchcraft—how did you get it?*

M C: *I don't have any knowledge of witchcraft. It reminds me of a story that happened when I was writing* Tituba. *Two students from the Occidental College newspaper asked me for an interview about my current writing. I told them I was writing about a witch. After that I was flooded with calls from people saying they wanted to meet me to discuss witchcraft. One day a lady came to my office by surprise and said, "I wanted to meet you because I myself am a witch." I had to say, "I'm sorry, I'm not a witch myself, I'm just writing about a witch, but I don't have any knowledge of witchcraft." The recipes that I give in the novel are merely recipes that I found in seventeenth-century books: how to cure people with certain plants, what kind of prayers to say in certain circumstances, and so on. I found that in books printed and published in America or in England.*

A S: *The concept of positive sorcery is central to the text. Can you comment on that?*

M C: *In Africa, as you may know, the word* witchcraft *has a different meaning. In any given community, you have two types of individuals relating to the invisible forces. The first type is working for the benefit of the society, i.e., is working, as they say, with the* right *hand. The second type is working evil on the individuals and the community. It is said that this type is working with the* left *hand. Only the second person is called a witch and is ostracized. Tituba was doing only good to her community. Could she be called a witch? I don't think so, and the book is there to prove it.*

A S: *And the concept of positive love is also central to the text?*

Afterword

M C: *It seems to me that love is always positive. If you love somebody, you are there to help the person, to give the person warmth and everything that she or he might need.*

A S: *Am I correct in believing that you favor independence from France for Martinique and Guadeloupe?*

M C: *I do. I do because it seems to me that we are mature enough in Guadeloupe and Martinique to look after our own destiny. We have so many talented and competent people that we can really take charge of our countries. We are the last colonies of France in the Caribbean. Everybody else is independent. Even small places like Dominica, like Barbados, have a measure of independence. I don't see why we can't have the same. I'm fed up with writing "nationalité française communauté économique-Européenne" (French citizenship, European Economic Community) on my passport. It seems to me that I'm living in a kind of vacuum, and that being a Caribbean person, I would love to have a nationality that expresses my environment, my history, and my reality.*

A S: *What is your reaction to writing in Creole?*

M C: *Formerly, we French-speaking West Indians, we used to despise Creole. We did not believe that it was a language, rather a dialect, unworthy of educated people. Times have changed. We now believe that Creole is a very important element of our culture, and we have reevaluated it. Although I do not see myself writing in Creole, living in Guadeloupe, I have modified my use of the French language and integrated in it many Creole expressions. However, I fear that Creole might become a prison in which the Caribbean writers run the risk of being jailed. According to the subject and the setting of my novels, I want to remain free to include in my language the amount of Creole that I desire. Some beautiful writings in Creole exist, notably by a Martinican poet called Monchoachi, the late Sonny Rupaire.*

A S :   *You have spoken in interviews of your life as a girl and the relationship between that experience and your writing. Are there new influences from your adult life that you would like your readers to hear about now?*

M C :   *I shall simply say that your life constantly impinges on your writing. My new experiences in America will certainly shape my future novels.*

A S :   *How is your journey back to Guadeloupe feeling at this point? Was writing* Traversée de la mangrove *an important step into full Guadeloupean reality?*

M C :   *I do not know what it is to be a full Guadeloupean and what you mean by "full Guadeloupean reality." If there is something that I discovered when I settled in Guadeloupe it is that a writer should never settle anywhere. Looking for one's native land, dreaming about it, doing everything to go back, that is a fantasy, a myth. Once one is there, one realizes that one has only one desire: to leave. I dare say that a writer should be perpetually on the move, going from one place to another, searching, trying to understand and decipher things different and new all the time. I came back to settle in Guadeloupe. However, after three years I am already teaching half of the time in Berkeley. I discovered that* root *is a very negative word. It ties you down.* Traversée de la mangrove *just illustrates a stage in my literary development. From there I shall certainly move on.*

A S :   *The relationship between men and women continues to be a central theme of your work. How do you view contemporary society in terms of women's independence?*

M C :   *I'm surprised to hear that, because I don't see myself as portraying the relationship between men and*

*women. There is never anything dogmatic or didactic
in my thoughts. Of course men are difficult, especially
Caribbean men, difficult to handle. In* Tituba, *I had
the factual story that John Indian deserted Tituba. So
I could not tell anything else. I had to take that historical factor into account. But I won't say that I'm
portraying the relationship between men and women.
If I do, it is totally unconsciously.*

A S: *In a speech you gave in Haiti and that was published
in the review* Conjonction, *you said that you learned
"race does not exist, only cultures exist."*[8] *Could we
say that in* Tituba *you portray a "culture of women?"*

M C: *When I say that race does not exist, only culture, I
express my viewpoint about negritude. It was simplis-
tic to believe that all the blacks throughout the world
were alike. Frantz Fanon was the first to warn us
that there are not two identical cultures and that the
Negroes were an invention of the white world. I mean
by this that the culture of the diaspora has become
very different from the one of the mother continent.
There is nothing aggressive in this affirmation. I am
just stating a fact. As for a culture of women, as you
say, I do not know whether it really exists. Certainly
women share a common oppression and a common
discrimination throughout the world. But this should
not obscure the oppositions created by social class,
education, ideology, and environment. What is more
different than a woman from rural Mali and a woman
from Milwaukee for example?*

A S: *Would you say that racism is a more central issue in*
Tituba *than discrimination against women?*

M C: *Of course, racism is very important in* Tituba. *She
was forgotten by history because she was black. But*

---

8. Maryse Condé, "Note sur un retour au pays natal," *Conjonction* [Port-
au-Prince, Haiti] 176 (1986): 7–23.

it seems to me more important that she was forgotten because she was a woman. She was a black woman. It seems to me that I stress her condition as a woman more than I stress her condition as a black. John Indian, who was as black as she was, managed to find a way out of the common plight. So the book is more about the discrimination and the ruthlessness against women than against people of color in general.

A S: *You also said in the speech in Haiti published in* Conjonction *that what makes an individual a Caribbean writer is not clear. Are you any closer now to an answer to that question than you were?*

M C: *I am not at all closer to an answer. When I am in Guadeloupe, I often discuss Caribbean identity with my friends. Some believe that its basic element is the knowledge of Creole. Having lived outside Guadeloupe for so long, I don't really use Creole in my daily life. So I don't agree with them. Some argue that it is dancing. I know a host of people who just like me are not particularly fond of either the* zouk *(modern new music of the West Indies), the* gwo-ka, *or the beguine. Others say that it is food and cooking. For me culture is something that cannot be rationally defined. There is no clear definition of either a West Indian person or a West Indian writer. One feels West Indian because of a particular relationship to oneself, to one's environment, to the rest of the world. This feeling is nurtured by a particular history and sociology. But there is no directory of how to be a true West Indian.*

A S: *Which of your novels do you like best and why?*

M C: *That is a question that you should never ask, because a novelist cannot like his or her novels. They are so far from the ideals in mind that it is a constant disappointment to reread them. But I must say that I like* Hérémakhonon *because the destiny of the novel is peculiar. I like it because it was so adversely re-*

viewed, misunderstood, unjustly criticized. I also like Traversée de la mangrove *because it is the latest. It is like a newborn child. You don't know exactly what the destiny of the child is going to be, which means you have to protect him, to be there, to help him to walk and move and talk. Maybe I would say the first and the last of my novels are my favorites. But probably I shall prefer the novel that I am now writing to* Traversée de la mangrove, *because it will become the latest in a few months.*

A S : *If American readers of* Tituba *were going to read only one other of your works, assuming they too will become available in English, which one would you like them to read and why?*

M C : *They could read either* La vie scélérate *or* Traversée de la mangrove. La vie scélérate, *because it is my own story and my family's story with, of course, the distortion of fiction. So if they want to get to know me, they might read that novel. And* Traversée de la mangrove, *because it is the last, as I said. Also it seems to me that in terms of writing techniques and narrativity, it is better than the others.*

A S : *If Caribbean readers were to read just one other of your works, which one would you choose?*

M C : Traversée de la mangrove, *because it is closer to their reality. I wrote it when I was in Guadeloupe. They will find some realities that they are familiar with.*

A S : *I know you are tired of hearing about women writers who are inspired to write because they heard their grandmothers tell stories. However, it seems to me that in* Tituba *you emphasize the intergenerational connections. Is there a way in which you are inventing a tradition for yourself?*

M C : *The question of grandmothers telling stories and thus teaching their granddaughters how to become writers*

*is one of the biggest clichés of black female writing.
I repeat that the element of parody is very important
if you wish to fully comprehend* Tituba. *As I am very
conversant with black female literature—I wrote an
essay called* La parole des femmes—*I know that in
any female epic, some elements must be present, and
I deliberately included them. If one misses the parody
in* Tituba, *one will not understand, for example, why
she meets Hester Prynne in jail and why they discuss
feminism in modern terms. Similarly, the presence of
the invisible (the conversations with the mother and
with Mama Yaya) is deliberately overdrawn. Do not
take* Tituba *too seriously, please.*

A S: *Are there other French Caribbean writers who have
influenced your writing? Who are they, and what
particular influences do you ascribe to them?*

M C: *No writer from the Caribbean has influenced me. I
already said how much I admire Aimé Césaire. But I
won't say that he influenced my writings. For me, he
was a kind of ancestor figure who opened my eyes and
probably brought me to literature. If I have to find
some writers who influenced me, I shall mention the
French writer François Mauriac, the American writer
Phillip Roth, the Japanese writer Mishima. Recently
I read a novel that was so important to me by Bruce
Chatwin called* The Viceroy of Ouidah. *I found it fas-
cinating. It seems to me that the novel was telling the
same story as* Ségou: Les murailles de terre *and* Ségou:
La terre en miettes, *but with an economy of means, a
kind of power of expression, a kind of terseness that
I still have to discover. I'm not influenced by any par-
ticular writers of the Caribbean. I take my influence
from everywhere.*

A S: *What are you working on now?*

M C: *I cannot tell.*

Afterword

A S: *How do you manage to be so prolific?*

M C: *Just because I have a lot of ideas.*

Maryse Condé does not merely retell Tituba's story; she recreates it to new purposes. Part of the fiction resides in the author's affirmation that "Tituba and I lived for a year on the closest of terms. During our endless conversations she told me things she had confided to nobody else." Condé's primary purpose in this text is to shift the focus to Tituba's personal power as a woman and as a human being. In doing this, she allows her heroine to subvert racial and sexual domination by the double Other (socially established whites / selfish men), and she empowers her readers to throw off their own chains as well. But Condé has an important secondary purpose that may appear to be at odds with the social-realist notion of a "message." As she suggested in our interview, she was conscious of creating a work of postmodern fiction that defies the norms of mimesis. The ways in which style and narrative strategy impinge on meaning in *I, Tituba, Black Witch of Salem* will be addressed following consideration of the dual issue of racial and sexual domination.

Tituba is an energetic, compassionate, gentle, and loving person who embraces life in a spirit of innocence. Unlike Maryse Condé's other protagonists, Tituba's whole essence is deeply tied to a celebration of being a black Caribbean woman. Her beliefs about religion and her intimacy with the natural world express the Barbadian half of her origins. Her openness toward other people is a sign of her humanity.

The title of the novel, *I, Tituba, Black Witch of Salem*, introduces the major themes that Condé will develop in her version of the story of the historical Tituba. Her use of the phrase "I, Tituba," shows us that Condé is claiming a life, an identity, for this woman in no uncertain terms. Making this even clearer, the French title uses the emphatic pronoun *moi*, drawing attention to the speaker: *Moi, Tituba, sorcière . . . noire de Salem*. The word *I* also tells us that Conde's Tituba will tell her own story.

This first-person narrative point of view empowers the heroine, making her a survivor rather than a victim, and it invites
the reader to become much more intimate with the protagonist. Such intimacy is essential to another of Condé's ultimate
purposes, to make us feel as deeply as possible the injustice of
history's treatment of Tituba.

In putting "Tituba" in the title, Condé emphasizes the importance of naming, of calling into being, thus linking up with
a theme that has become central to literatures of the previously
dispossessed in which writers are re-visioning the group's lost
history. One recalls Mircea Eliade's discussion of myth and the
need for cultures to retell their own stories in order to keep
their traditions vibrant and alive. One is equally reminded of
Edouard Glissant's contention that the opaque void of past
history must be filled in where it can be.

The text of the novel also emphasizes the importance of naming. Tituba explains that she got her name from Yao, the slave
to whom her mother, Abena, is given when the new master
realizes she is pregnant: "Then, holding me up by the feet, he
presented me to the four corners of the horizon. It was he who
gave me my name: Tituba. TI-TU-BA. It's not an Ashanti name.
Yao probably invented it to prove that I was the daughter of his
will and imagination. Daughter of his love." This explanation
explores the importance of love in the midst of a plantation
space characterized by the Other's hatred at the same time that
it proclaims Tituba's significance to the world. Yao thus demonstrates real power of his own, even though he is a slave.
Condé explains the name of John Indian, Tituba's future husband, by imagining for him a father who was an itinerant
Arawak Indian. Emphasizing the fact that Condé's versions
of naming are consistent with the multicultural history of the
Caribbean region, Clarisse Zimra adds that they claim an identity for Tituba untainted by her father's English heritage rather
than perpetuating the power of the dominant white masters.
The text of *I, Tituba, Black Witch of Salem* is framed by two
historical references: a few lines from the Puritan poet John
Harrington at the beginning and a historical note of one page
at the end. The poetry, which embodies the Puritan notion that

life is supposed to be endured rather than enjoyed, foreshadows the pain and suffering that will occur in the lives of Tituba and the Puritan women whose domestic servant she becomes. The message in the poetry also works in juxtaposition to Tituba's own tendency to find joy in life and to be cheerful whenever she can.

The historical note at the end of the text, which is indeed factual in every respect, authenticates the witch-trial proceedings incorporated within the novel itself.[9] Designed to enhance the verisimilitude of the story, the historical note also emphasizes the fact that Condé is speaking to two audiences, those who know American history and those who don't, and it shows how limited was the information she had to work with. The name Salem in the title affirms the "reality" of a specific period of American history, and it further inscribes the narrative in a particular American locale. The other elements of the title, *Sorcière . . . noire,* meaning "witch" and "black woman" in French and translated into English as "Black Witch," accord with Condé's revised focus in that they establish the importance of Tituba's race, gender, and life calling as a healer at the outset.

The text itself speaks of filling in the voids of recorded history. Late in the narrative, Tituba cries out in anguish as she thinks ahead into her historical future:

As I stumbled forward, I was racked by a violent feeling of pain and terror. It seemed that I was gradually being forgotten. I felt that I would only be mentioned in passing in these Salem witchcraft trials about which so much would be written later, trials that would arouse the curiosity and pity of generations to come as the greatest testimony of a superstitious and barbaric age. There would be mention here and there of "a slave originating from the West Indies and probably practicing 'hoodoo'." There would be no mention of my age or my personality. . . . I would never be included! Tituba would be condemned forever!

9. See Francis J. Bremer, *The Puritan Experiment: New England Society from Bradford to Edwards* (New York: St. Martin's Press, 1976): 165–68.

Afterword

There would never, ever, be a careful, sensitive biography
recreating my life and its suffering.
 And I was outraged by this future injustice that seemed
more cruel than even death itself.

In this passage Condé draws attention to her own impetus for
writing the novel, reminds us that historians have paid almost
no attention to Tituba, and condemns Puritan New England.
At the very end of the novel the reader discovers along with
Tituba that her story does indeed live on, in Caribbean folk
song . . . and in the novel we have just finished reading.

 The mock-epic quality of *I, Tituba, Black Witch of Salem*
is evident in anachronisms and cultural inconsistencies in the
text. While incorporating African "roots" into this pluricul-
tural narrative, Condé subverts history for her own purposes.
For instance, the tribal wars between the Ashanti and the Fanti
that Tituba mentions actually occurred in the 1800s, not the
1600s.[10] American readers will be sensitive later in the novel
to the anomaly that occurs when Tituba meets Hester Prynne,
Nathaniel Hawthorne's heroine in *The Scarlet Letter* (1850).
Just as importantly, this encounter with a fictional character
undercuts any possible verisimilitude. Condé's Hester, who is
pregnant, befriends Tituba in jail and later commits suicide
there, whereas Hawthorne's Hester gives birth to little Pearl
and then lives out her life in Salem after Arthur Dimmesdale's
death. In all of this subversion of history, Condé frees herself to create a fiction with multiple layers of interpretation
that invites richer resonances with the reader's own literary
experience. Historicity works on both the collective and the
individual level as the story of the Middle Passage and its
American aftermath is expressed through the telling of Tituba's
personal story.

 Beginning her tale with the events of her own conception,
Tituba tells us that her Ashanti mother, Abena, was raped by
a white sailor on the slave ship *Christ the King*. Tituba's conception and birth are a metaphor of the English slavers' rape

10. "Empire of Ashanti," *Encyclopaedia Britannica,* 1981 ed.

of the African continent. The rape of Abena portrays men's domination over women and the ship's name shows the irony of Christian religious practice in a society where slavery is a mainstay. Finally, the rape of Abena dramatizes the nature of Tituba's mulatto heritage. She is biologically African and European and, like the New World whose history she will help to mold, she was born of violence.

From the outset, style and narrative strategy impinge on the reader's consciousness in this novel. When Tituba tells the story of her birth, the style is jarring and disjointed. This lack of fluidity in the text forces the reader to recognize Tituba's own ambivalence about her origins. Furthermore, the fragmentation is expressive of her broken mulatto heritage. The choppy narrative style of the first few pages also makes the reader experience a related discomfort. One wonders if the novel will even be worthy of attention, because it seems unworthy of perusal, like Tituba's life. It is significant that, when Tituba moves away from the plantation to live with the natural healer Mama Yaya, she becomes infused with the African part of her heritage. The narrative becomes more fluid as Tituba integrates herself into the land, and the reader settles in for a good story.

Using a distinctly Caribbean geography—silk-cotton trees, calabashes, flamboyants, the Ormond River, Carlisle Bay— Condé tells the story of Tituba's childhood in Barbados, contrasting harsh facts of life on the slave plantation with the love and warmth of human connections. She makes us feel the humiliation and anger Tituba herself feels in the presence of Susanna Endicott, her new mistress. Condé describes how this woman and her friends talk about the new slave, Tituba: "It was not so much the conversation that amazed and revolted me as their way of going about it. You would think I wasn't standing there at the threshold of the room. They were talking about me and yet ignoring me. They were striking me off the map of human beings. I was a nonbeing. Invisible. More invisible than the unseen, who at least have powers that everyone fears. Tituba only existed insofar as these women let her exist. It was atrocious. Tituba became ugly, coarse, and inferior because they willed her so."

218

Afterword

Although Condé explores certain aspects of Tituba's character such as her compassion, her sensitivity to her own sexuality, her ability to love, and her fierceness about being mistreated, she makes it clear that Tituba does not control her own life. A. James Arnold suggests that this refusal to allow Tituba's life to be deeply independent permits us to deconstruct the social and economic system of slavery that tied the British West Indies to North America in the seventeenth century.[11]

The emphasis on Tituba's religious/spiritual powers in the narrative enhances Tituba's status as a folk heroine and makes the useful point that there are different ways of interpreting the world. However, it is clear that Condé has exaggerated these details consciously and intends to challenge the credulity of her readers, once again denying verisimilitude to her own text.

At first, Mama Yaya initiates Tituba into a philosophy of life she will later share with others, exemplifying a natural religion based on an intimate knowledge of nature and life: "Mama Yaya taught me the sea, the mountains, and the hills. She taught me that everything lives, has a soul, and breathes. That everything must be respected. That man is not the master riding through his kingdom on horseback." The focus on animism becomes exaggerated only after numerous explanations are given, and even then it is appealing material. Mama Yaya says: "The dead only die if they die in our hearts. . . . They are all around us, eager for attention, eager for affection." These thoughts refer to the African animist belief that death is a passage, a metamorphosis from life to spirit. Once the ancestor becomes a spirit, she or he no longer leaves the living, but participates in their lives.

Furthermore, Tituba learns that the canal of dreams is a passageway between the dead and the living, and that women in particular have special religious powers with which they can sometimes bring the spirits of the deceased back to living form.

11. A. James Arnold, "Poétique forcée et identité dans la littérature des Antilles francophones" (Forced poetics and identity in the literature of the francophone Caribbean), in *L'héritage de Caliban / Caliban's Legacy* (Basse-Terre, Guadeloupe: Editions Jasor, 1992).

Afterword

Later on, Tituba conjures up the presence of her spirits, her deceased mother and Mama Yaya, seeking advice from them and taking comfort in their nearness to her in times of trouble. She can make them appear at will by uttering incantations and offering the appropriate sacrifice (unless they are across the sea, as we learn). Tituba also conjures up Abigail, the deceased wife of Benjamin Cohen d'Azevedo, permitting the bereaved husband to speak with her. Because the reader of *I, Tituba, Black Witch of Salem* is not likely to believe that the dead can reappear and speak to the living, the repeated instances of this activity quite consciously undercut the plausibility of the text, even though the reader may welcome the relief from loneliness and suffering that the spirits offer the characters.

Tituba's entire life is a demonstration of the power and importance of love. Her sense of humanity is all the more dramatic and powerful for being set against the background of tyranny and hatred of difference that flourished in Puritan New England. Tituba approaches others with openness and compassion in spite of her bondage. She remains loyal to John Indian even after he deserts her because his own life is threatened. The importance of love is reiterated three times near the end of the novel: Benjamin Cohen d'Azevedo gives Tituba her freedom because he loves her deeply; Tituba accepts the passion of Iphigene's affection for her even though he is young enough to be her son; and she decides not to abort the child that is growing within her. She expresses the healing, vital power of love: "Blessed is the love that carries man on the waters of oblivion. That makes him forget he is a slave. That rolls back the torment and the fear. Reassured, Iphigene and I plunged back into the healing waters of sleep. We swam against the current watching the needlefish court the crayfish. We dried our hair under the moon."

One of the essential ironies of *I, Tituba, Black Witch of Salem* is that Tituba is indeed a sorceress, but a life-giving one rather than the demon-linked creature she is accused of being by Samuel Parris and the Puritan tribunal. Tituba uses her powers of healing on numerous occasions; she eases the pain of the Reverend Mr. Parris's sickly wife, she cares for Benjamin

Afterword

Cohen d'Azevedo's nine children, she heals the wounds of the maroons in Barbados.

The cruel treatment Tituba receives at the hands of the Puritan ministers and doctors illuminates their bigotry, insensitivity, and sexism, contrasting sharply with Tituba's own kindness. Condé uses graphic details with relentless clarity, searing the reader's imagination with pain, just as Tituba experiences the pain in her body:

> "One of the men sat squarely astride me and began to hammer my face with his fists, which were as hard as stones. Another lifted up my skirt and thrust a sharpened stick into the most sensitive part of my body, taunting me: "Go on, take it, it's John Indian's prick."
>
> When I was nothing more than a heap of suffering, they stopped, and one of the four spoke up again.

Here exaggeration is used for shock value that dramatizes the intensity of the scene.

On the one hand, Tituba incarnates the quality of "goodness" in the sense in which Condé explains it in *La parole des femmes;* certain people are inaccessible to evil, because they know how to act against it. These women possess spiritual and therapeutic abilities that they use for the benefit of the community. They practice witchcraft for good purposes and have an important place in society. This gift of healing is not something one can seek; it is instead bestowed on the individual. On the other hand, Tituba seems too good to be true, in that she refuses to use the weapons of her accusers to protect herself from their attacks. Much as we admire her, the person Condé creates really *is* too good to be true; one wonders how anyone could possibly be as forgiving as Tituba is in such traumatic circumstances. Hence, she becomes a mock-epic protagonist, her goodness magnified beyond belief.

Tituba's life with the maroons once she returns to Barbados recreates an important part of Caribbean folklore. In Condé's novel, however, a double irony creates more parody. Tituba's lover, Christopher, the leader of the maroons, is actually in league with the plantation owners and lives in freedom on the condition that he reveal the names of others who foment rebellion. Christopher, whose name recalls that of the ship on which Tituba was conceived and hints at martyrdom as well, eventually becomes the instrument of his own ignoble death.

Unlike Ann Petry's Tituba in *Tituba of Salem Village,* who is presented as a victim most of the time, and unlike Arthur Miller's Tituba in *The Crucible,* who criticizes Puritan society but plays a small role in the play, Condé's Tituba takes charge of her own life in a fuller sense. After Mama Yaya dies and the plantation is sold, Tituba chooses to live alone and manages to do it well until she meets John Indian. Her first willful act in the novel is her desire to make this man love her. The force of Tituba's active approach to life works in part as a metaphor, demonstrating that the old tradition of listening to others' versions of history must end, that it is time to act. It is also through her own energy that she later infuses healing into those around her.

Condé embeds a distinctly feminist language in the narrative at this point. Considering what has happened to Abena, the language seems quite appropriate at first. Mama Yaya tells Tituba: "Men do not love. They possess. They subjugate." The feminist language gets much stronger, surfacing again when Tituba talks with some of the Puritan women and coloring all of the conversations she has with Hester Prynne. For instance, Hester tells Tituba: "I'd like to write a book, but alas, women don't write books! Only men bore us with their prose. I make an exception for certain poets. Have you read Milton, Tituba? Oh, I forgot you don't know how to read. *Paradise Lost,* Tituba, a marvel of its kind. . . . Yes, I'd like to write a book where I'd describe a model society governed and run by women! We would give our names to our children, we would raise them alone."

Another narrative strategy that impinges on the reader's consciousness in this text is parody. For starters, Condé's title is an obvious echo of the title of the very successful *Moi, Joséphine, impératrice* (I, Josephine, empress) by Paul Guth, which the Paris publisher Albin Michel released in its "Mémoires Imaginaires" (Imaginary memoirs) series in 1979. In the passage where Yao names Tituba, Condé has appropriated the famous naming scene in Alex Haley's *Roots*, in which Kunta Kinte (on whom Yao is so manifestly patterned) names Kizzy. These details all become part of the mock-epic texture of the novel, which gradually takes on for the reader self-evident intertextual resonances.

Condé points out in our interview that Arthur Miller does not pay a great deal of attention to Tituba in *The Crucible*. He does indeed portray Tituba as a black slave woman who speaks pidgin English, who stammers out her love for "her Betty," and who makes the girls drink chicken's blood. However, he also gives her a subtle power by making her a critic of the Puritans' devil. Her sarcasm in suggesting that the Puritans hear the mooing of a cow when they say they hear the devil talking is clear: "TITUBA: Oh, it be no Hell in Barbados. Devil, him be pleasureman in Barbados, him be singin' and dancin' in Barbados. It's you folks—you riles him up 'round here; it be too cold 'round here for that Old Boy. He freeze his soul in Massachusetts, but in Barbados he just as sweet and—*A bellowing cow is heard, and Tituba leaps up and calls to the window:* Aye, sir! That's him, Sarah!"[12]

Miller addresses other issues that preoccupy Condé as well. Both writers describe the rising level of hysteria that characterized the witch trials and accusations, they examine moral right and wrong in the New England Puritan society, and they castigate the narrow-minded, hypocritical Puritan attitude toward those who are not of their persuasion. Condé emphasizes Abigail's precocity and deceit, while Miller focuses on her commission of adultery with John Proctor.

What is perhaps most interesting is that both Condé and Miller use the Salem witch trials of the seventeenth century to attack the social circumstances of their respective decades in history. Condé's *I, Tituba, Black Witch of Salem* cannot be read without the thought that elements of America in the 1990s are every bit as frightening—the resurgence of the Ku Klux Klan, the bigotry of skinheads, the gang warfare in our

12. Arthur Miller, *The Crucible* (New York: Bantam, 1959), p. 117.

cities, not to mention Condé's own statement in our interview about the extent of racism in the United States today. It may seem paradoxical that Condé, a foreigner from another region of the Americas, should open our "American" eyes to the rigidity and brutality of Puritan times as well as suggesting to us metaphorically what is wrong in the United States today.

Miller makes clear—in one of the prose passages inserted in *The Crucible*—his intention of linking the Salem witch trials in 1692 with the Communist witch-hunts of the McCarthy era in the 1950s: "A political policy is equated with moral right and opposition to it with diabolical malevolence. Once such an equation is effectively made, society becomes a congerie of plots and counterplots, and the main role of government changes from that of the arbiter to that of the scourge of God. . . . The Church, sharp-eyed as it must be when gods long dead are brought to life, condemned these orgies as witchcraft and interpreted them, rightly, as a resurgence of the Dionysiac forces it had crushed long before. Sex, sin and the Devil were early linked, and so they continued to be in Salem, and are today." [13]

Just as the creation of *I, Tituba, Black Witch of Salem* symbolizes renewed ties to the Caribbean for Maryse Condé, so the novel includes fundamental patterns of birth and rebirth. The rhythm of re-creation runs through the plot, as Tituba brings life back into the languishing body of Mistress Parris, as she nurtures little Betsey's desire for attention, as she chooses to bear the child of her maroon lover, Christopher, and as she heals the maroon women, her potential rivals.

Tituba herself is reborn three times in the text. First, at her own trial, she manages to be faithful to her personal code of ethics. From a kind of death in which she has been flooded by doubts about her ability to stand firm, she rises up and maintains her personal integrity by refusing to give in to temptations to do evil and accuse innocent people. Second, she comes alive again when she establishes a loving, compassionate relationship with Benjamin Cohen d'Azevedo, after he takes her into

13. Ibid., pp. 32–33.

his home. Finally, she returns to Barbados at the end of the novel and creates a new life there, experiencing a kind of rebirth as she uses her healing powers and accepts the rhythm of the days: "I discovered how to treat these illnesses. I also discovered how to treat yaws and to heal those wounds the slaves got day after day. I managed to mend open, festering wounds, to put pieces of bone back together again, and tie up limbs. All that, of course, with the help of my invisible spirits, who hardly ever left me. I had given up the illusion of making men invincible and immortal. I accepted the limits of the species."

Tituba's historical death and her subsequent rebirth under Condé's pen suggest renewed spiritual resources. The fact that Tituba reaches a place of inner peace and balance in Barbados before she dies offers hope for younger generations. The novel would seem to come full circle when Tituba is hanged, as her mother was. However, the reader's outrage at this final injustice combines with the lessons of love, endurance, and rebirth Tituba has taught by example throughout the novel. The ethical thrust of the story—which Condé's narrative strategies conspire to question at every turn—suggests the possibility of breaking the circle of hatred, prejudice, and violence. One need not accept the plot device of Tituba's life as a spirit after death—indeed, the style suggests that Condé does not expect us to accept it as "truth"—in order to take comfort from her story.

Compassion and parody, then, emerge as the double hallmark of *I, Tituba, Black Witch of Salem*, a novel that is considerably more complicated than it seems on first encounter. If love informs Tituba's way of being in the world, parody inhabits Condé's creation of a mock-epic protagonist. Her postmodern and intertextual play on other literary works draws the reader into an opaque literary universe where nothing is fully defined but much is scrutinized. In that ambiguous universe the reader finds that the doors for future discoveries about self and society are wide open.

Like so many good novels, this one affords an opportunity to confront personal prejudices as well as to plumb human nature. Condé's cross-cultural subject matter is sometimes very

Afterword

disturbing. That very feature extends an invitation to explore one's own limitations. I myself was embarrassed to realize that I had missed the element of parody on first reading because I was so eager to celebrate Tituba's heroism and her Caribbean-ness. Wanting to honor the novel for its "ethnicity," I ended up missing part of the point, as Maryse herself helped me discover. Furthermore, I was shocked to learn through our May 1991 interview that I was attributing Tituba's generosity of spirit to the fact that she was Caribbean rather than to her stature as a human being! I do not especially like to see my own prejudices in operation, but that is the principal way we learn that they exist. My purpose in bringing them to the attention of future readers in this essay is to suggest that others may experience similar revelations through their experience of this fictional version of history. Finally, in the matter of prejudices, it is pertinent to remind ourselves here that *I, Tituba, Black Witch of Salem* is partially the result of Condé's having conquered the prejudice against her Caribbean background instilled in her by her own parents when she was a child. Would that all such victories were so fruitful!

Bibliography

Principal Works by Maryse Condé

Fiction

Hérémakhonon. Paris: Union générale d'éditions, 1976.
————. Rev. ed. *En attendant le bonheur.* Paris: Seghers, 1988.
Une saison à Rihata. Paris: Robert Laffont, 1981.
Ségou: Les murailles de terre. 2 vols. Paris: Robert Laffont, 1984.
Ségou: La terre en miettes. Paris: Robert Laffont, 1985.
Pays-mêlé. Paris: Hatier, 1985.
Moi, Tituba, sorcière . . . noire de Salem. Paris: Mercure de France, 1986.
La vie scélérate. Paris: Seghers, 1987.
Traversée de la mangrove. Paris: Mercure de France, 1989.
Les derniers rois mages. Paris: Mercure de France, 1992.

Theater

"Le morne de Massabielle." (Unpublished first play; world premiere, Paris, at Théâtre des Hauts de Seine, 1972; premiere in English trans. at Ubu Repertory Theater, New York City, November 1991.)
Dieu nous l'a donné. Théâtre africain. Paris: P. J. Oswald, 1972.
La mort d'Oluwémi d'Ajumako. Théâtre africain. Paris: P. J. Oswald, 1973.
"Les sept voyages de Ti-Noël." Written in 1986; unpublished.
Pension les Alizés. Paris: Mercure de France, 1988.
"Comédie d'amour." Written in 1989; unpublished.

Essays

La poésie antillaise. Classiques du monde. Paris: Nathan, 1977.
Le roman antillais. Classiques du monde. Paris: Nathan, 1977.
"Cahier d'un retour au pays natal" [de] Césaire. Profil d'une oeuvre. Paris: Hatier, 1978.
La civilisation du bossale. Paris: L'Harmattan, 1978.
La parole des femmes: Essai sur des romancières des Antilles de langue française. Paris: L'Harmattan, 1979.
L'héritage de Caliban / Caliban's Legacy. Edited by Maryse Condé. Guadeloupe: Jasors, 1992.

WORKS BY MARYSE CONDÉ
IN ENGLISH TRANSLATION

Heremakhonon. Trans. Richard Philcox. Washington, D.C.: Three Continents Press, 1982.
Season in Rihata. Trans. Richard Philcox. Portsmouth, N.H.: Heinemann, 1987.
Segu. Trans. Barbara Bray of *Les murailles de terre.* New York: Viking, 1987.
The Children of Segu. Trans. Linda Coverdale of *La terre en miettes.* New York: Viking, 1989.
The Hills of Massabielle. Trans. Richard Philcox. New York: Ubu Repertory Theater Publications, 1991.
Tree of Life. Trans. Victoria Reiter. New York: Ballantine, 1992.

Caraf Books
Caribbean and African Literature
Translated from French

Serious writing in French in the Caribbean and Africa has developed unique characteristics in this century. Colonialism was its crucible; African independence in the 1960s its liberating force. The struggles of nation-building and even the constraints of neocolonialism have marked the coming of age of literatures that now gradually distance themselves from the common matrix.

CARAF BOOKS is a collection of novels, plays, poetry, and essays from the regions of the Caribbean and the African continent that have shared this linguistic, cultural, and political heritage while working out their new identity against a background of conflict.

An original feature of the CARAF BOOKS collection is the substantial critical essay in which a scholar who knows the literature well sets each book in its cultural context and makes it accessible to the student and the general reader.

Most of the books selected for the CARAF collection are being published in English for the first time; some are important books that have been out of print in English or were first issued in editions with a limited distribution. In all cases CARAF BOOKS offers the discerning reader new wine in new bottles.

The Editorial Board of CARAF BOOKS consists of A. James Arnold, University of Virginia, General Editor; Kandioura Dramé, University of Virginia, Associate Editor; and three Consulting Editors, Abiola Irele of the University of Ibadan, Nigeria, J. Michael Dash of the University of the West Indies in Mona, Jamaica, and Henry Louis Gates, Jr., of Harvard University.